THE MEDIA
AND POLITICS

Other Books in the At Issue Series:

THE MEDIA
AND POLITICS

David Bender, *Publisher*
Bruno Leone, *Executive Editor*

Scott Barbour, *Managing Editor*
Brenda Stalcup, *Series Editor*

Paul A. Winters, *Book Editor*

An Opposing Viewpoints ® Series

Greenhaven Press, Inc.
San Diego, California

Library of Congress Cataloging-in-Publication Data

The media and politics / Paul A. Winters, book editor.
        p.   cm. — (At issue) (An opposing viewpoints series)
    Includes bibliographical references and index.
    ISBN 1-56510-383-1 (lib. : alk. paper). — ISBN 1-56510-382-3
(pbk. : alk. paper).
    1. Mass media—Political aspects—United States. 2. United
States—Politics and government—1989–   . I. Winters, Paul A.,
1965–   . II. Series. III. Series: Opposing viewpoints series
(Unnumbered)
P95.82.U6M45   1996
302.23'0973—dc20   95-39053
                                                                         CIP

302.23
M

c. 1

© 1996 by Greenhaven Press, Inc., PO Box 289009,
San Diego, CA 92198-9009

Printed in the U.S.A.

Table of Contents

Introduction

"Why, after more than three decades of steadily increasing apathy and hostility toward the electoral process, did Americans in electing Bill Clinton and denying George Bush a second term post the largest percentage turnout since the election of John F. Kennedy?" This is the question posed by Jack W. Germond and Jules Witcover in *Mad As Hell: Revolt at the Ballot Box, 1992*, their account of the presidential election. In fact, an estimated 55.24 percent of the voting age population (including 11 million first-time voters) participated in the 1992 election, according to the Committee for the Study of the American Electorate—an increase from 50.1 percent in 1988 and a turnout larger than any since 1972. The higher turnout raised the question of why American voters, whose participation had steadily declined since 1960, showed increased interest in this particular election.

For Germond and Witcover and other media experts, part of the answer lies in the role the press has come to play in campaigns and in the utilization in the 1992 election of "new media"—talk shows, cable television shows, 800- numbers, and the expanding network of computers, electronic mail, and fax machines. They argue that both voters and candidates had become increasingly frustrated and turned off in the past by negative campaigns. Many identified the "old media" as the source of their frustration, complaining that the traditional newspapers and network news shows focused too much on "character" issues, scandals, and polls rather than the economic and political issues most important to voters. The new media offered beleaguered candidates the opportunity to bypass the old media and spread their unfiltered campaign messages to voters, according to Germond and Witcover, and "enabled the candidates . . . to tap directly in to the voters' frustration . . . and to give it an outlet." More important, they contend, the new media allowed voters to voice personal concerns and questions to candidates and become directly involved in the election. Voters "had been quiet long enough. They had turned their backs on the political process long enough," explain Germond and Witcover. "They demanded to be heard . . . through whatever electronic means were available to them."

The problems of the old media

In their study of voter attitudes toward the media and politics the Twentieth Century Fund Task Force on Television and the Campaign of 1992 reported, "Negative politics, attack advertising, and rough press coverage seemed to reach a new level of pervasiveness during the 1988 presidential campaign." According to the task force, voters cited the "Willie Horton" ads produced by Bush supporters as a prime example of the reasons for their frustration with politics. These commercials featured a black prison inmate who committed violent crimes while participating in a furlough program implemented by Bush's opponent, Massachusetts governor Michael Dukakis. The ads were criticized for cynically playing on voters' fear of crime and on racial tensions while offering no positive or substantive information about Bush. In reaction to the increasingly negative nature of campaigns, newspapers such as the *New York Times* and *Washington Post* and network organizations such as ABC and NBC news made a pact, prior to the start of the 1992 race, to try to raise election coverage to a more constructive level. They vowed to critically evaluate the content of campaign ads and focus on economic and social issues.

However, despite the old media's vow to focus on issues, the 1992 campaign seemed destined to frustrate voters in the same way that the 1988 race had. In January 1992 major newspapers and network news shows aired allegations first made by a weekly supermarket tabloid, the *Star*, about a twelve-year extramarital affair between candidate Bill Clinton and Gennifer Flowers, an Arkansas state employee. The allegation produced a "feeding frenzy" among the media, with news organizations competing to provide lurid details of the scandal. The media appeared unable to resist focusing on character issues, and the majority of voters, who were more interested in political and economic issues than the Flowers scandal, said in polls that they felt as alienated from the electoral process as ever. In the task force's words, "The emphasis on gossip, scandal, trivia—what's called 'tabloid journalism'—was decried by citizens, politicians, scholars, and media representatives themselves." Many media critics believed that the scandal was indicative of a chronic problem with the old media's role in elections. In the opinion of political scientist Thomas E. Patterson, author of *Out of Order*, the old media had become "a barrier between the candidates and the voters rather than a bridge connecting them."

Some media scholars defend the role of the old media. They maintain that, despite the Flowers controversy, coverage of the 1992 campaign was significantly better than in 1988 and showed that it was possible for the media to improve the quality of their reporting. Marvin Kalb, director of the Joan Shorenstein Barone Center on the Press, Politics, and Public Policy at Harvard University, states, "There is no doubt in my mind that television coverage of the 1992 campaign was better than anyone had expected." Kalb and others argue that, overall, campaign reporting by newspapers and traditional news shows focused on the issues and provided important information to voters. Everette E. Dennis, executive director of the Freedom Forum Media Studies Center, contends that the old media "did quite a good job [in 1992] with critical fact-checking" and investigative reporting.

The promise of the new media

Looking for solutions to the problems of the old media, some observers saw in the use of the new media in the 1992 election a revolutionary way of connecting frustrated voters with political leaders. As political scientists Edwin Diamond, Martha McKay, and Robert Silverman put it, "With so many people telling the public opinion pollsters that they are angry and alienated, [candidates] would be foolish not to use as many means as possible to reach turned-off voters." According to these media observers, the new media "helped transform American politics. Both our leaders and citizens are instantly in touch by radio, television, and '800' numbers." By giving voters a forum to question candidates for themselves and a chance to evaluate for themselves the direct statements of the candidates, they contend, the new media promoted voter involvement and participation. In the "talk show campaign" of 1992, as Diamond, McKay, and Silverman enthusiastically labeled it, "the public became part of the process, an active participant." The newly elected president, Bill Clinton, who many felt made the best use of the new media throughout the campaign, agreed that these new communication forums had helped him to reach voters and to win the election. In his inaugural address, he told voters, "You have raised your voices in an unmistakable chorus, you have cast your votes in historic numbers, and you have changed . . . the political process itself."

Other campaign observers dispute that the new media brought about a revolutionary change in the election process. Thomas Patterson argues, "Although the candidates' 1992 efforts to go around the press were described as a new development by some observers, the same thing had happened in 1984 and 1988, when the Reagan and Bush campaigns had based their communication efforts on televised political advertising." A number of reporters and media experts warn of problems with the new media, particularly in cases where candidates use it to bypass the old media. For instance, the Twentieth Century Fund task force contends that although direct communication between politicians and voters is beneficial to the electoral process, many new media formats allow candidates to lie to or intentionally mislead voters because no reporters are present to ask probing or clarifying questions. In its report, the task force notes that "these new entertainment outlets often fail to recognize their responsibility to the public, not just to ratings, when interviewing candidates." Reporter and media critic Ken Auletta defends the role that the old media plays in elections. He states, "We need an intelligent press as a filter. If we [in the old media] are to be that filter, we have to win back the public trust that we've lost."

Most media experts agree that the new media will be a permanent part of the campaign process. The question for future presidential elections is what effect, if any, the new media will have on voter participation. *At Issue: The Media and Politics* explores the relationship between the emergence of the new media and voter involvement in the political process.

1

New vs. Old Media in the 1992 Presidential Election: An Overview

The Research Group of the Freedom Forum Media Studies Center

The Freedom Forum is a nonpartisan organization in Arlington, Virginia, that promotes freedom of speech and of the press. Its Media Studies Center, located at Columbia University in New York City, is an institute for the advanced study of mass communication and technological change. The Research Group was formed to study the 1992 presidential campaign.

In the 1992 presidential election, candidates and voters seemed to favor "new media" such as talk shows and MTV over traditional media such as newspapers and network news. Journalists and scholars disagree as to why the new media played such a prominent role in the election and whether this will be a feature of future campaigns. According to some, the new media offered voters direct access to the candidates and a greater sense of political participation than traditional media—a change they believe is positive and likely permanent. Others argue that voters turned away from traditional media only for the time being because these sources missed important stories—such as the rise of Ross Perot and racial issues—and focused too heavily on polls, controversies, and scandals. Most agree that the possible negative aspects of the new media have not been sufficiently examined.

Editor's note: The following panel of journalists and scholars met several times during the 1992 presidential campaign to discuss the role of the media. The discussion here took place on November 13, 1992, ten days after the election.

Ken Auletta, a former fellow of The Freedom Forum Media Studies Center, is a journalist and author. Alan Brinkley is a professor of history at Columbia University in New York City. Jannette Dates, a fellow, is an associate professor in the department of radio, TV, and film at Howard University in Washington, D.C. Everette E. Dennis is head of the Research Group of The Freedom Forum Media Studies Center. Margaret Gordon, a former senior fellow, is dean of the Graduate School of Public Affairs at the University of Washington in Seattle. Henry Graff, a former senior fellow, is a professor of history at Columbia University. Lawrence Grossman, a former senior fellow, is the past president of NBC News and PBS. Jerry Hagstrom, a former research fellow, is a contributing editor of the *National Journal*. Mark Jurkowitz is a media critic for the *Boston Phoenix* newspaper. John McMillan, a former fellow, is retired publisher of the Utica, New York, *Observer-Dispatch*. Patricia O'Brien, a former fellow, is a journalist, author, and former press secretary to Michael Dukakis. Charles Overby is president and CEO of The Freedom Forum. Adam Clayton Powell III, a former fellow, is a producer for Quincy Jones Entertainment. David Stebenne is a lecturer in history at Yale University in New Haven, Connecticut.

Looking ahead to future political campaigns, the 1992 presidential race contains many important lessons for the media, some of which will affect the public's tolerance for the traditional press's filtering effect on political news. There is good news and bad news for the press in the aftermath of the 1992 campaign: On the one hand, the public demonstrated a level of interest and sophistication concerning the political process that frankly surprised media people, who are accustomed to playing the gatekeeper role. On the other hand, much of the public's attitude throughout the campaign seemed to be that the press not only couldn't be trusted to deliver untarnished political news, but had become irrelevant to the process once new, less filtered avenues for political information became available.

The final meeting of the Center's panel of media and political experts, professionals and scholars [on November 13, 1992,] just ten days after the election was marked in many ways by a sobering recognition that change, possibly irrevocable change, had occurred in the media-candidate-public triad in 1992. For some, such as former NBC News and PBS President Lawrence Grossman, the changes of 1992 were positive, harbingers of a more involved and activist public in a participatory democracy. For others, however, such as journalist and author Ken Auletta, the public's desire to eliminate the middleman in 1992 was a vote against the news media that may represent a future, permanent diminution of the press's importance in public affairs.

The public vaulted over mainstream media and started getting information in a way that made them feel they were getting better *information.*

It may be that the election of 1992 was an anomaly, a year of political mavericks and news-as-entertainment that will fade and not be repeated. On the other hand, the panelists suggested, Ross Perot demonstrated that it might be possible to buy a presidential election, and the media's lack of scrutiny of the Perot "curiosity" was an example of an old-line press's failure to perform its watchdog role in a new political context.

There seems little question that the media dynamic is unlikely to evaporate with the election of Bill Clinton, who as president surely will continue to take his message directly to the people, just as he did as a candidate. In this way, the direct link between politician and public that revolutionized electioneering in 1992 may well revolutionize how Americans are governed in the future.

Good news–bad news

EVERETTE E. DENNIS: The obvious place to begin is by discussing what happened with the media's campaign coverage and why. There seem to be two points of view on the media in this campaign. One is very positive, even somewhat self-congratulatory: Didn't the press do a good job this year? Isn't it better than in the past? The other one is that the media were unfair.

Another area to examine is whether the changes we've seen in this race will be lasting or ephemeral. One such change is the rise of direct-access media. Are we whistling in the wind when we focus attention on what are seen as the respectable, important media—newspapers, news-magazines, network news—without thinking also about the role that talk shows, MTV, databases and other media played in the campaign and will play in the next four years of a Clinton administration and in future campaigns?

KEN AULETTA: One thing that happened this year may be ephemeral and another may not be: There was the vote on Election Day, but throughout the campaign there was another vote, and I think that was a vote against the media.

The public expressed itself in many ways, through "Larry King Live" and the network morning call-in shows. They weren't happy with the role we were playing in our new role as party chiefs who replaced the parties after the 1970s [McGovern-Fraser Commission] reforms. People figured out ways to get around us and were encouraged in doing so by candidates who saw that was in their best interests.

What may be ephemeral from this year is the increase in public interest in serious issues that we saw throughout the campaign as evidenced in the ratings growth for discussion of politics. In general, that interest level has not been present in previous presidential campaigns. What I think is permanent, though, is the effort of people to interact directly in the process. That's what happened, in fact, in Eastern Europe when they overthrew the middleman, the socialist government; it's what we see happening with home banking, home computers and the mail-order catalog business; what we see in TV clickers that give us the choice of what we want to watch and when we want to watch it. Throughout our society, we are seeing a move to get rid of the middleman. That's what happened this year in politics.

Effectively, they didn't eliminate the middleman in the election, of course, because the press will always play the middleman. But the media's role will forever be different and less prominent. That's both good and bad.

PATRICIA O'BRIEN: I agree that there have been changes this year, but the word "permanent" always bothers me when it applies to anything in politics, because "permanent" usually has a way of lasting four years or maybe a maximum of eight. The most intriguing question for the media right now is how they respond to the fact that the public vaulted over mainstream media and started getting information in a way that made them feel they were getting *better* information.

ALAN BRINKLEY: I think we have to look at the various interests that are involved in this change that Ken was talking about. The public really did have an interest this year in circumventing the mainstream media and seeking other sources, but there are two other interests involved: the candidates and the media themselves.

Candidates have always wanted to get on television as much as possible. So once it became acceptable for them to get on programs other than the Sunday morning talk shows and the news, it opened up a huge new possibility for free television time in all sorts of different markets. Candidates are going to be very reluctant to turn away from that.

That's one reason I think Ken is right that this is one change that's going to last. But then we have to balance that against the institutions of the media themselves, which have no obligation to have candidates on talk shows as often as they did this year. They did so because politics suddenly was so popular, but in another election, with other candidates in whom public interest is less high, it may be that Larry King won't be as eager to have these people on his show as often.

So judging how permanent this will be requires evaluating how all these different interests are going to respond to this change. I suspect it *will* be a lasting change but one that varies from one election to the next.

Untold stories, untouched issues

HENRY GRAFF: There are a number of things that suggest issues in this campaign that we haven't examined very well.

For instance, the mainstream press is singing the praises of Clinton. Well, that's fair enough, but they've become part of the new administration very quickly. What happened to Gennifer Flowers? She's in *Penthouse* this month [November 1992], and I have not seen any commentary on that. I'm not suggesting the press ought to repeat the intimate details of what she alleges were her relationships with men and particularly with the president-elect. But it *is* a news story—have the media collectively decided that they were sorry they dealt with Gennifer Flowers in the first place?

I also notice that we have not fully analyzed how this campaign went. Here you have two Southerners and they don't carry the whole South—wasn't there a racist element operating here? Joe Califano, in his last book [*The Triumph and Tragedy of Lyndon Johnson: The White House Years*], says Lyndon Johnson said that if the Civil Rights Bill of 1964 passed there wouldn't be a Democrat in the White House in our lifetime. Clinton and Gore carried Georgia by a whisker. Race was not discussed in this campaign; it almost does not exist any longer on the agenda. It didn't come up at Clinton's press conference yesterday [November 12, 1992]. It's unspoken.

MARK JURKOWITZ: Unfortunately, Henry, I can answer your question about Gennifer Flowers. In my other life as a radio talk show host, we actually had her on, much to my chagrin, the last weekend of the campaign, after the *Penthouse* story had come out.

Penthouse actually did a fairly balanced piece in which questions about her character were seriously raised. As a result, Gennifer Flowers is now anti-media. I can officially tell you that. She said *Penthouse* did not fulfill its promise to let her see the piece after it was done, and she was very upset with the way it turned out. So we now have another person who hates the media.

I think the press has to think about its obsession with insider questions, which was another thing that the public voted against this year.

HENRY GRAFF: There is another area I think we haven't looked at closely enough—the Perot vote. If Perot hadn't been on the ticket, for whom would people have voted? That whole Perot phenomenon requires much closer examination. It's pointed out in this week's *Economist* that 30 percent of the people in Maine voted for Perot; that was also where Jerry Brown did well. Is that nut country? What is going on? And how do we explain it?

DAVID STEBENNE: Thinking about the media's overall performance in the last leg of the campaign, I am struck, too, by their failure to explain the Ross Perot contribution. In retrospect, I think historians will view Ross Perot as *the* creative element in the election.

The debates were the most interesting and the most watched ever, largely because Ross Perot participated and—I don't think this has ever happened before—he assisted his rival Bill Clinton in getting over the top. At the end of the campaign, the media assumed that Ross Perot would fade, because third-party candidates always fade. But he was able to spend so much money on advertising that he didn't fade but actually rose in the last two weeks. Throughout the campaign, he was the variable no one anticipated. His entry in the first place changed the race; his re-entry did the same.

I don't think the media did a very good job in reporting on Perot; they wrote about him and did their own version of Gennifer Flowers on him late in the campaign, but that was their principal contribution. Perot drew people to the polls who would not otherwise have voted, thereby raising turnout, and took votes away from the GOP. Those are the two things that made possible the biggest and the most decisive Democratic victory in over a quarter of a century.

HENRY GRAFF: There's probably some exhaustion on the part of the press, but they also don't know what to write about. I just had a call from the Sarasota paper, and the reporter said, "Look, I'm here covering Bush's vacation. He's going to fish four or five days. Will you talk to me about what other presidents did with their spare time?" Clearly, there's work to be done, and it is not being done.

MARK JURKOWITZ: We in the media will have to make some internal changes in the language we use and what we focus on.

The second debate before the 209 so-called "real Americans" in Richmond, Virginia, had a very interesting dynamic. Everybody in my busi-

ness—everybody who's an insider, everybody who's in the media and politics—*hated* that debate. Their response was, "She asked a dumb question," or "What she *meant* to ask was 'How does the *recession* affect you?'
not 'How does the national debt affect you?'" And they said, "Those were
powder-puff questions. How dare that guy cut Bush off when he was going to . . ." I mean, the journalists wanted a fight and everybody was upset with how soft and squishy it was. Sure, there were dumb questions.
But everybody *outside* of this business that I talked to liked that debate;
everybody said it was really interesting.

A positive aspect of the "new news" is that it gets away from the language and the constructions the press uses. A couple of days after Clinton
was elected, I saw an NBC report with Andrea Mitchell. She said he was
going to create a council of economic advisers, like the security council.
Obviously, the entire country wants something done about the economy.
But the NBC piece focused on the mechanics and the internal politics—
How could three different layers of bureaucracy work together? And
whose ox will be gored and who won't get along with who, and what
kind of political problems will it create for the administration? This is not
what real people were talking about.

A lot of the "new news vs. the old news" debate is about the media's
way of looking at things. I think the press has to think about its obsession
with insider questions, which was another thing that the public voted
against this year.

LAWRENCE GROSSMAN: We're still underestimating what has really happened. In the first meeting we talked about something very fundamental
going on in the drift of the so-called "new news."

---

*When [news is] related to the African-American
community and it's not something about decadence
and despair, . . . then it's just ignored.*

I think there's been a real revolution that has broken down the sepa-
ration in this country between politics and the rest of life. Traditionally,
there was the political campaign and then the period when it's all over;
the media focused on politics and then there was the rest of the world.
Now what you have is politics involving everything from the entertainment shows to the late-night talk shows and so on. You have the rise of
direct democracy, which was Ross Perot's great contribution. No longer
do the parties pick the candidates; it is the primaries that do that now.
You have the rise of direct initiatives and more money spent directly lobbying people for political change than lobbying state legislatures. And the
"new news" is a natural extension of all that.

We're going to see politics extending itself between elections,
through town meetings, through public debates and through people re-
quiring Clinton and the opposition to get on TV and present issues. It's
becoming integrated into all of life and this election campaign was a sort
of high spot in making that happen. I think we've seen a sea change in
the nature of politics in society.

It's not just that the press's role was downplayed, but I think a direct engagement of all of society in the political sphere has occurred, which I think is quite a profound movement.

Race and the '92 campaign

JANNETTE DATES: We've got young people involved in politics for the first time in years, and I hope that is a permanent change. I think it might be; I don't know how anyone can run for president again and not go to a venue like MTV and make certain that you tie in with that group of people.

In the context of race in this campaign, I think African Americans looked at Clinton after all those years of being very unhappy with the Reagan-Bush White House and realized that in many ways Clinton was the best hope for them. Although one could argue that someone running for president should court those people whom he wants to support him, African Americans felt they did not need to be unhappy about the fact that he was not approaching them in this manner. They would have liked it, but they went for him because they knew that he offered things that other people had not offered them all these years.

EVERETTE DENNIS: Do you have any idea why Jesse Jackson went off the news coverage radar screen during this campaign?

ADAM CLAYTON POWELL III: A lot of the events with Bill Clinton and Jesse Jackson, certainly those events two weeks before the election, were timed deliberately to come after the mainstream press's deadlines, so that they would only run in the black press and not in the mainstream media. Those events were timed for late night or, as somebody put it, for all the Saturday afternoon newspapers out there.

JANNETTE DATES: There was also the strong feeling that if anyone stressed race issues too heavily, Clinton and Gore would lose so much of the white suburban vote that they would lose the election. I think black people were conscious of that. Democratic Party Chairman Ron Brown and Clinton were certainly conscious of it.

EVERETTE DENNIS: That doesn't explain why the press wasn't covering some of it.

MARK JURKOWITZ: The Joan Shorenstein Barone Center on the Press, Politics and Public Policy at Harvard has looked at evening news clips and coverage of the candidates appearing with white crowds, with mixed-race crowds and with minority crowds. The records across the board are abysmal. Clinton showed up on evening news clips in mixed crowds about 25 percent of the time and in all-black crowds just 5 percent of the time.

Clinton's use of visuals in this campaign—and his advance team was very, very aware of it—was critical to the success of his campaign with suburban white voters in general, and with the American people in general. The strategy was a page out of the Reagan playbook in many respects.

JANNETTE DATES: Clinton spoke at the National Association of Black Journalists (NABJ) convention in Detroit last summer [1992] and was asked really strong questions, and he responded quite well. Yet there was no coverage of that. Though the media were there covering the convention, there was nothing in the press. The news gatekeepers must have decided it was not an important story.

I'm struck by the fact that this is often the case—when it's related to the African-American community and it's not something about decadence and despair, or entertainment, or sports, then it's just ignored.

Obviously, this is something that needs to be looked at in terms of what's going on in urban centers across the country and how the media cover them. Deciding what's important comes from your individual frame of reference; we need frames of reference that include more people other than those who have made news-coverage decisions through the years, who think it's not news unless it's decadence or despair.

ADAM CLAYTON POWELL III: Just a little background on how the Clinton campaign structured that day: He went straight from the NABJ stop in the morning to the Detroit Economic Club for his major event of the day. And they structured it so that that would be the major speech the press reported and to marginalize the NABJ appearance.

That's what they did whenever he appeared in the South. During the last two weeks, he appeared with Jesse Jackson and members of the Congressional Black Caucus at voter registration and "Get Out The Vote" drives. They were structured so those would not be the events that dominated the day's news, so that there would be other things that would be reported about Clinton.

Polls closings and the West Coast

JOHN MCMILLAN: From the perspective of a small state on the West Coast [Oregon], I have three footnotes having to do with the public's view of the media filter. First, Jackson campaigned in two cities—Medford and Eugene—in a state that is as white as any state in the country. It was reported fully in the press and it was very visible in Oregon.

Second, we talk about radio talk shows and we talk about the various direct-access television programs. At least in Oregon, in the midsized and smaller papers, there were far more letters to the editor than usual—this is anecdotal, not statistical—to the point where some papers stopped running editorials, dropped all their columnists and just ran a page or two of letters to the editor.

Third, the national media decided the biggest issue was the presidential contest. But in Oregon, more people voted in state contests; people there cared more about disenfranchising gays than they did about the presidential race.

MARGARET GORDON: I think that this thing in Oregon and the fact that more people voted there on Proposition 9 [a proposal to bar homosexuality as a category for civil rights protection] than for the presidency may have been affected by the fact that, by 6 p.m., Clinton was projected as the winner and that he was going to be the winner in Washington, Oregon and California. I heard all kinds of stories about people standing in line to vote just turning around and walking out. But in Oregon, they stayed to vote on that one issue.

People very much resented the East Coast media projecting the winners before the polls had closed in their time zone. It could have had a very bad effect on the state and local contests.

PATRICIA O'BRIEN: The media unfairly takes that hit. That's something the Senate has to decide; I think there should be a uniform poll-closing time. It goes against everything we're trained to do to sit on the results and not say what they are.

JERRY HAGSTROM: I can't imagine that voters on the West Coast would be very happy to be told to stop going to the polls at an earlier hour to satisfy reporters' desire to report the news.

LAWRENCE GROSSMAN: As somebody who still has the scars from lashes on his back from this very issue, let me say that I thought that this election night was obscene in that sense. Everybody, out of the side of his or her mouth, was trying to tell us the inside stuff. It's got nothing to do with reporters, it's got to do with the fact that the information is available and that nobody's going to get it for three hours.

To say that you have to wait until polls close on the West Coast or in Hawaii to find out if your local mayor or city councilman has been elected is just absurd. Either we have to have a total ban on any coverage of the election at all until every poll is closed—because it's going to slip out; everybody in the media knows from his own polls and the only ones who won't know are the people—or we have to have uniform poll closing. That's the only way to solve that problem.

KEN AULETTA: I wonder if we let the press off too easy on this question. There is a clear, legitimate issue as to whether the public is being intruded upon when media, particularly television, kind of winks and tells audiences who is winning.

It's a problem because the press, if it knows something, wants to report it. That's our job. But I wonder if we don't do the equivalent in reporting polls throughout the campaign—the way we cover polls and our preoccupation with the horse race. I think that's one of the things the public resents, that we're telling them it's over two weeks before Election Day, according to the polls. We spend so much time reporting polls that, in a way, it becomes the equivalent of reporting exit polls early on election night. It feeds that impression of the arrogant, insider press who is interested in suppressing the voters and not allowing them to make their own decisions, to see the candidates and sift and weigh the evidence themselves.

I wonder whether this is not a subject we ought to be a little more cathartic about as reporters, and look at whether our need to have the arrogant, all-knowing pose—to tell you what's happening—has not drifted over and now covers things like horse-race coverage and polls.

Covering a new administration

PATRICIA O'BRIEN: Postelection coverage tells us something about ourselves we need to know. The week after the election was an absolute news vacuum. You have some 75 reporters or so down in Little Rock, Arkansas, whining because they have no stories, getting increasingly angry at a very sensible decision by Clinton to keep his mouth shut, to make no plans and no decisions.

It was a very sensible thing for there to be a quiet week, but we have seen a great deal of coverage that showed us something of the arrogant base that we operate from, which is—we want news, give it to us. A story on the front page of the *New York Times* comes to mind, about the suddenly minimal news out of Little Rock. The article was so cranky and seemed to scream, "Where is my news? I want my news!"

I think that tells us something about ourselves, how we react when there is a news vacuum. It gives us a better image of ourselves in a year when there has been news coming at us from every angle.

EVERETTE DENNIS: You mentioned the politicians were tired in the last two weeks of the campaign. Is the public also tired? And is the press out of sync in thinking that there needs to be an equally dense amount of material immediately after the election. I saw some stand-up reporters in Little Rock being asked by the desk in New York when will the president-elect appoint his cabinet. And they said, "Well, he'll certainly have to make some major appointments by the end of next week."

No president-elect has appointed cabinet members ever until December and often in January. And yet there's now this heightened expectation that news has to be constantly generated.

JERRY HAGSTROM: I'm struck that, with all these reporters sitting down in Little Rock saying that they want their news, how little analysis we have. For instance, after all this effort, after this extraordinary campaign, why did Clinton get only 44 percent of the vote? And I had no idea that Clinton was doing events with Jesse Jackson after the news deadlines. Where were the stories about Jesse Jackson and Bill Clinton campaigning after hours?

I'm also taken by the lack of analysis over the fact that Bill Clinton did not win his own region, the South. When times get tough, he won't be able to go to the senators and congressmen in his own region with any assurance that they will support him. Bill Clinton's real constituency is in big states in this election—California and New York. And if he doesn't reward California, possibly at the expense of the South, he may not get that vote again in four years. To my mind, his coalition is very soft in parts of the country where he's not a native. And yet, we haven't had much analysis of this.

And finally, I've seen very little postelection analysis of what the 19 percent Ross Perot phenomenon means and what kind of a club this is going to be over the Clinton administration. I was in California last weekend for a meeting of the International Association of Political Consultants, and one of the Perot people spoke there about how they were going to continue to get organized and open a Washington office within 90 days. Perot is giving them what he calls "bridge money" until they can form their organization.

I think a lot is going on out there in politics while these reporters are all sitting in Little Rock wanting to report who the new cabinet members are. To me, it's extremely lazy, compared with going out around the country and really getting stories.

Polls and pleasing the public

ALAN BRINKLEY: We've heard around the table today and elsewhere two very different criticisms of the way the media have performed.

One is a kind of populist criticism, that the media aren't giving the public what it wants. Ken suggests the horse race, the polls, the frilly reporting on election night, the talk show phenomenon are all evidence of the media's failure to give the public what it wants. The people liked the soft debate rather than the hard debates.

The second criticism is that the media aren't being tough enough, that the media aren't going after the tough stories, that they've been too soft on Clinton since the election, that they aren't asking questions that should be asked, even though there's no opportunity for them to be asked.

Those are very different and incompatible criticisms. They suggest that there is a dilemma about what the press's role should be that was accentuated during this campaign. Should it be to please or should it be to inform? Or should there be some balance between the two? I, for one, think that the media's role is to inform, whether or not the public likes it.

Although I perhaps agree with Ken that the way the media reported polls this campaign season was not always the best, polls do exist, candidates do use them and every media organization has them. I think it would be both dishonest and wrong not to report them. I would say the same about the reporting on election night, which made me extremely uncomfortable—the smirking, artificial reporting, knowing full well that everybody knew more than they were telling.

I don't think the media's role is to please the public. When they know things, they should report them. When they think questions are important, they should investigate them.

KEN AULETTA: I think it is true that there is often a contradiction between the desire to please and the desire to inform. Please don't interpret what I said earlier as a suggestion that we're in the business of pleasing.

I do think, however, that we would please more if we informed more. That is to say, I think we give too much attention to polls—there's too intense a preoccupation with them. One of our great failures is we don't try more to *inform*. I think if we did that, the public may be bored with some of it, but our job is to provide information. I think we'd please them more if we did that, more than with this often mindless preoccupation with polls and the horse race.

I think that's one of the things the public resents,
that we're telling them it's over two weeks before
Election Day, according to the polls.

LAWRENCE GROSSMAN: I don't believe that public interest in politics has ended with the election results. This goes back to the integration of politics into real life. I think we had a view that everybody turns off the election as soon as the political season is over, and that the best place to educate people about issues is during a political campaign. I think we're going to find that it's much more effective to educate them out of the election season, because there are so many issues and they are so complicated.

In terms of actually developing a public appetite to find out about the real issues—health care, welfare reform, education choice—education is going to have to go on after and between election seasons. That's where the media, I think, must reshape their thinking about priorities to deal with those kinds of issues. I think there's a real public appetite for that now.

MARK JURKOWITZ: This year the media raised the preoccupation with polls to ridiculous heights. I think that in the last two weeks of the campaign, polls manufactured a completely bogus dynamic for this election.

When everybody was satisfied that they had looked at enough polls to figure that Clinton was going to win, *Newsweek* made him president of the United States.

The other dynamic was this tightening of the campaign, because CNN had changed the way they were polling people not to include people who had not voted in Gallup, to get the race within one point. This false tightening of the race drove the story for days. By the end of the campaign, having once again opened up the way they were polling, the last day, CNN had a gap of 12 points. So you were supposed to believe there was an 11-point move in the last week of the campaign.

In this race, with everybody—partisans or media people—really paying attention, we were on a roller coaster that was probably completely manufactured by daily tracking polls, by the screens that were used that drove a completely phony story. I think that needs to be looked at next time around.

Debate coverage and media fairness

EVERETTE DENNIS: Something we've touched on here before is the issue of traditional forms and measures of news judgment—whether it's politics or something else—versus the desire to balance and project an image of fairness in coverage.

That was the criticism in 1988 as well. Now comes a report, not from one of the right-wing or left-wing media evaluating groups, but from Nexis, a division of Mead Data Central, and PR Data Systems. The report says this: "An independent survey of stories and headlines about the presidential debates has concluded that the reporting was riddled with biased writing, most often favoring Bill Clinton at the expense of President Bush. News articles before and after the three debates held in October gave Mr. Clinton favorable treatment 48.4 percent of the time, compared with 29.7 percent for Ross Perot and 21.9 percent for President Bush, the survey found. The negative coverage for Mr. Bush occurred 71.9 percent of the time, of Mr. Clinton, 15.3 percent, and of Mr. Perot, 12.8 percent, according to the survey released yesterday."

Nexis and Mead Data Central, of course, have no vested interest in offending anybody; they want to sell their service. So this isn't Accuracy in Media or Fairness and Accuracy in Reporting or one of those groups.

Do people care about fairness in the old partisan sense or should we evolve a new definition of fairness if we're getting these kinds of report cards from essentially neutral organizations?

LAWRENCE GROSSMAN: I have a lot of trouble with that kind of analysis. If you're a journalist and you're reporting on something that everybody has seen, the only way to have a neutral report is to regurgitate what everybody has said, which is a total waste of time, so that what you get is analysis or perspective or, really, subjective reporting—who won, who lost, who was smarter, who was dumber, who was articulate, who was not, who answered the questions, who avoided the questions. It may very well be that the press was biased in its reporting, but I suspect that particular statement had more to do with what went on in the debates than whether the press comes in with a bias in favor of one candidate or another.

In answer to the general fairness issue, one notion that I don't think is expressed enough is how powerful and influential the media are. I thought the job done on Ross Perot really changed an awful lot of public opinion of who Ross Perot was and what he was all about.

There's now this heightened expectation that news has to be constantly generated.

JERRY HAGSTROM: I was struck that during the general election campaign, no press stories seemed to me to be as important as either seeing the debates themselves or Ross Perot's paid advertising. Those two things, to me, were the story of what happened in politics from September onward.

I don't know how much coverage of the debates mattered this time because so many more people watched them, twice as many as in 1988. And here's another interesting phenomenon to consider: How do you evaluate media coverage of something that so many people see?

HENRY GRAFF: What are the assumptions when the debates finally are announced and both sides have agreed on all the details? Is the assumption that there are millions of people out there waiting to listen to the arguments of the three participants and *then* they will make up their minds?

All evidence points to the fact that people make up their minds very early; I don't know who or where this great undecided group is. I don't know about your experience, but I didn't run into people who were undecided.

Most people I talked to—"real Americans," I guess—had made up their minds very early. They were tired of the campaign and they were looking ahead to the Superbowl. Meanwhile, we keep following this in detail, taking the temperature of the candidate twice a day. I have a feeling that we overestimated the value of the debates. We didn't hear anything new in any of them. And I don't believe that late revelation about Weinberger's notes on what Bush knew had any effect at all on the campaign. Can you imagine millions of people saying, "Oh! Now I will vote for Clinton because Bush has lied to us"? I see no evidence of that.

MARGARET GORDON: I don't know if I agree, Henry. We have talked about the media positioning themselves between the candidates and the people. It seems to me that these talk shows, and to some extent, the debates and, certainly, the infomercials let the candidates finish sentences and express a full idea, in a way that the people really, really liked. The people think they can judge for themselves about a person's character if they get a chance to hear enough sentences from him. That's why these techniques, including the debates and their new formats, were so popular.

Most people didn't feel they knew Perot and Clinton very well and they wanted a chance to see them for themselves. I think the public thought that if it could see the person on television and look at him as he answers a question, they could tell for themselves what they think.

MARK JURKOWITZ: Henry, this is the year that it paid to be an undecided voter, because if you told the press you were undecided at the last minute, you had TV cameras pointed at you and notebooks in your house.

But am I the only person who thinks that Ross Perot came dangerously close to getting away with murder with the media? Because if we recall the circumstances under which he dropped out, there were a series of fairly damaging stories at that point, many of which connected him to Nixon and just shattered the image of him as an outsider. Others dealt with his lack of knowledge of the issues, which arguably, he may have overcome.

But he got out of the race and then came back in at the end—the political version of Rosie Ruiz, the woman who did the same in the Boston Marathon—with $60 million to get out an undiluted message. I think the man was essentially treated as a curiosity by the press, but not as a man who could have been president of the United States. And that was very, very dangerous.

When the Stockdale debate occurred, we all either recoiled in horror or felt sorry for the guy [James B. Stockdale was Perot's running mate as candidate for vice president]. Where were the stories about who would populate a Perot administration? Frankly, it wasn't until Perot did it to himself, when he talked to "60 Minutes" and to the *Boston Herald* about his fears over his daughter's wedding—*that's* when the stories came out all of a sudden about the Black Panthers on his lawn.

That was a self-inflicted wound, but he came very close to running to the finish line with his $60 million without anybody in the media getting in his way.

I don't think the media's role is to please the public. When they know things, they should report them.

DAVID STEBENNE: The last time we met, Henry Graff said Clinton would win because people make up their minds by Labor Day. But the polls indicated that people were only weakly committed to voting before the debates and that many Clinton supporters were weakly committed to him. So what the debates did do, although they didn't change many minds, was firm up the general feeling of the electorate.

Debates are contests. If George Bush had been openly incoherent and called his opponents bozos during the debates and had suggested that he wasn't mentally competent, the coverage of his performance would have been even more negative. That, in itself, doesn't demonstrate any media bias at all. He *did* perform poorly; even the Republicans say that, and media coverage reflected it.

ALAN BRINKLEY: The Bush people complained that coverage of the Bush campaign was consistently suffused with the image of Bush losing. I think that's a fair characterization of the coverage. My impression of every story on the networks on George Bush was that it was another futile day in the Bush campaign, a note of gloom and defeat surrounding all the coverage of the Bush campaign.

The fact is that Bush *was* losing, so one could argue that this was accurate reporting. But I can't blame the Bush people for feeling they were treated somewhat unfairly. The whole tenor of coverage, it seemed to me, had a note of inevitability, of Bush losing—he didn't have a message, couldn't get his act together. Now, whether that's unfair in any absolute sense of the word, I don't know.

PATRICIA O'BRIEN: Part of the sense of defeat in much of the Bush coverage came, in fact, from a sense of doom and gloom at the White House. It was not just the media saying that things were falling apart in the Bush administration, it was the people who were working within the Bush administration. The atmosphere in the White House was grim; there was no sense of cohesion and no sense of focus. All that was truth, so if you're going to ask for balance and fairness, it will have to be balance of *that* truth.

ADAM CLAYTON POWELL III: The question then arises of how reporters and editors can be fair to a bad campaign, which is what the Bush campaign was. It was badly run and had bad strategy and tactics; it was inept, the candidate was inarticulate and the White House leaked gloom and doom. What *is* fairness to a candidate? Do you say, "Well, here's what he means. Here's what his argument *should* have been."

The press and the process

EVERETTE DENNIS: It was here at Columbia University that Paul Lazarsfeld did his famous "People's Choice" study on the 1944 election, which led to 50 years of American colleges and universities teaching their students that the media don't play an important role in politics, that the press may reinforce voters' beliefs, but it is not significant as a player that could change minds. I'm wondering if we'll have to call up Paul Lazarsfeld's ghost and tell him things have changed.

PATRICIA O'BRIEN: Although Henry is quite right about Iran-contra not making the slightest bit of difference in the vote for or against Bush, I do think that Leslie Stahl's piece on "60 Minutes" played a significant role in getting people to stop, step back and take a look at Ross Perot. His charge that the Bush people wanted to infiltrate his daughter's wedding gave us something that had been out there in tiny little fragments but had not been picked up. And that was that there was strong evidence that this man had strong paranoid tendencies.

Despite that sense, he got very far in this campaign. I wonder if in the future someone else might not try the same thing, the ploy of dropping out and then coming back out of the subway and running a last few yards, like Rosie Ruiz in the marathon. That strategy bought Perot great advantage. It took him out of the spotlight; he was not under scrutiny. When he came back, the news media were really busy, they had too many things to prepare and they weren't paying a lot of attention to Perot.

KEN AULETTA: At the outset of this discussion, I said I thought that the changes in direct access were both good and bad. We talked about some of the good; we haven't talked about some of the bad, the consequences.

The good is obviously a sense of empowerment; it's a major factor and the public feels more direct democracy.

The bad was a guy who came close to buying an election. He had some good ideas. He had a sense of populism, that he was against "them." But when he got back in the race, he did not appear before a reporter who asked questions for 23 days. Not only that, but he did not shake the hand of a voter for 23 days. He was a studio candidate. Bob Kerrey said to me that next time we could have a candidate who is going to learn from this year and figure out that he can not only bypass the parties, but bypass the press as well.

And next time, unlike Perot, it could be someone who really is much better informed on public issues. And you could well have some rich person come in and do that and not make the mistakes that Perot did. So when we talk about looking back at this campaign, we need to look at some of the things that are troubling about the new media and the new techniques of running, including watching Larry King interview George Bush and get confused between Iran and Iraq; not having the ability to follow up because he didn't have enough information to follow up. There are real negatives that we probably haven't given enough attention to.

LAWRENCE GROSSMAN: But, although I agree with you about Perot, can you imagine how terrible this election would have been without him? He really did serve as a catalyst; if we'd had to sit and watch Bush and Clinton go at each other for nine months, it would have really been another disastrous election year.

This is a great lesson of what the media's role should be. It may well be that if we are going down the road with this direct access and direct democracy, the press now can go back to its original function of critical importance, to be the commentator and the observer and not the central player, the way it has been so long in past elections and in past public affairs. The press's job is going to be to investigate, provide perspective and analyze all these knights on white horses that come on the screen and on the scene by virtue of money, character and access.

HENRY GRAFF: As we analyze this campaign process, as we look at all the bolts and look under the hood of this campaign, we lose sight that this whole process of choosing a chief is sloppy and cumbersome.

The people think they can judge for themselves about a person's character if they get a chance to hear enough sentences from him.

We have a new president from a third-world state about to take over the country, in the sense that Clinton comes from outside the system in many ways. It is remarkable that somehow, from all the United States, he was the best choice and, willy nilly, he emerged. In all our attempts to be scientific, we ought to take into account the mysterious way in which a large public chooses people.

CHARLES OVERBY: My overall impression concerns the bad news–good news aspects of this year's campaign. The bad news is based in this massive disenchantment by the public toward the media; I have never seen it any stronger than it is right now.

Beyond the perceptions, though, I think the words that describe this campaign best were Lawrence's—direct democracy, direct access. In such a direct-access democracy, there is an impression that the public doesn't need mainstream media to get news; that people can go to other sources. The public's day-to-day disaffection with the media in this campaign is short-term, because campaigns come and go, but it has more serious, long-term implications for readership, viewership and our whole news process.

Another important aspect of this campaign that we and the public struggle with is what Patricia brought up, the whole sense of balance in the media and how do you have balance when you're also supposed to report truth? I was with a major leader in the Bush campaign after the election, and he told me that from January forward, there was not one good day in the Bush campaign. He had been in many presidential campaigns and he said you always have your peaks and your valleys, but there was no peak in the Bush campaign from January forward. So how do you take all the bad days and have any sense of balance?

And finally, Henry talked about the sloppy process of electing a chief. All of us around the table have heard that there are two things that you don't want to watch being made—sausage and laws. We now have a third thing: the presidential campaign.

But even with all of these things and the negatives that go with them, the ultimate role of the media is to provide as much information as possible about the candidates so the public can make an intelligent decision. And when you grind out the sausage on November 3, the media did a pretty good job of giving the public information about the candidates so that they could go to the polls and elect a chief. So I end up on a positive note, but we have a lot to learn.

2

The Media Have Too Much Influence on Elections

Thomas E. Patterson

Thomas E. Patterson is a political science professor at Syracuse University in Syracuse, New York, and the author of many books on the mass media and American politics, including The Mass Media Election *and* The American Democracy.

Campaign reforms in the early 1970s changed the role of the media in elections. Prior to the 1968 election, presidential candidates were chosen by the political parties' leadership. Following the reforms of the McGovern-Fraser Commission, candidates were chosen by voters in primary elections. The unintended effect of the reforms was to give the media the responsibility of identifying viable candidates for president and informing voters about them. The media are ill-equipped to play this new role: Since they do not constitute a political institution, the media have no incentive to organize the demands of various interest groups and to attract votes, no coherent ideology, and no accountability to voters.

> The press . . . has come to be regarded as an organ of direct democracy, charged on a much wider scale, and from day to day, with the function often attributed to the initiative, referendum, and recall. The Court of Public Opinion, open day and night, is to lay down the law for everything all the time. It is not workable. And when you consider the nature of news, it is not even thinkable.[1]
>
> Walter Lippmann

The United States is the only democracy that organizes its national election campaign around the news media. Even if the media did not want the responsibility for organizing the campaign, it is theirs by virtue of an election system built upon entrepreneurial candidacies, floating voters, freewheeling interest groups, and weak political parties.

It is an unworkable arrangement: the press is not equipped to give order and direction to a presidential campaign. And when we expect it to do so, we set ourselves up for yet another turbulent election.

The 1992 campaign and the role of the press

The campaign is chaotic largely because the press is not a political institution and has no capacity for organizing the election in a coherent manner. The news can always be made better. Election coverage in 1992 was a marked improvement over 1988, and in a few respects the best coverage ever. The journalist Carl Bernstein, reflecting a widely shared opinion among members of the press, declared that 1992 coverage closely approximated "the ideal of what good reporting has always been: the best obtainable version of the truth."[2]

Yet news and truth are not the same thing.[3] The news is a highly refracted version of reality. The press magnifies certain aspects of politics and downplays others, which are often more central to issues of governing. During the last six weeks of the 1992 campaign, the economy got a lot of attention from the press, but it still received less coverage than campaign-trail controversies, including disputes over Clinton's draft record, Perot's on-again, off-again candidacy and spats with the press, and Bush's wild charges ("the Ozone Man," "bozos").[4]

The attention that Clinton's 1969 trip to the Soviet Union while a graduate student at Oxford received in the closing weeks of the campaign was in itself revealing of the gap between news values and the nation's real concerns. When Bush questioned Clinton's trip on CNN's "Larry King Live," it exploded into the headlines in a way that policy issues seldom do. News of Clinton's Moscow visit overshadowed such October issues as developments on the North American Free Trade Agreement, CIA revelations on the U.S. government's role in the arming of Iraq, and a change in Clinton's health-care proposal.[5]

The press's restless search for the riveting story works against its intention to provide the voters with a reliable picture of the campaign. It is a formidable job to present society's problems in ways that voters can understand and act upon. The news media cannot do the job consistently well. Walter Lippmann put it plainly when he said that a press-based politics "is not workable. And when you consider the nature of news, it is not even thinkable."[6]

Lippmann's point was not that news organizations are somehow inferior to political organizations but that each has a different role and responsibility in society. Democracy cannot operate successfully without a free press that is acting effectively within its sphere. The problem arises when the press is expected to perform the job of political institutions as well.

Election reform

The press's role in presidential elections is in large part the result of a void that was created when America's political parties surrendered their control over the nominating process. Through 1968, nominations were determined by the parties' elected and organizational leaders. Primary elections were held in several states, but they were not decisive. A candidate could demonstrate through the primaries that he had a chance of winning the fall election, as John Kennedy, the nation's first Catholic president, did with his primary victories in Protestant West Virginia and Wisconsin in 1960.

Nevertheless, real power rested with the party leadership rather than the primary electorate. In 1952, Senator Estes Kefauver defeated President Harry S. Truman, 55 percent to 45 percent, in New Hampshire's opening primary. Kefauver then won all but one of the other twelve primaries he entered, and he was the clear favorite of rank-and-file Democrats in the final Gallup poll before the party's national convention. Yet party leaders nominated Illinois governor Adlai Stevenson, in the process rejecting Kefauver, whom they considered a maverick.[7]

The nominating system changed fundamentally after the bitter presidential campaign of 1968. President Lyndon Johnson had entangled the nation in a war in Vietnam that seemed increasingly unwinnable. He was strongly challenged within his party by senators Eugene McCarthy and Robert Kennedy, which led Johnson to make a surprise announcement in a nationally televised address that he would neither seek nor accept his party's nomination. Kennedy's assassination in Los Angeles on the night of the California primary left McCarthy to carry the challenge, but he had lost several primaries to Kennedy and was regarded as a spoiler by party leaders. They nominated Hubert Humphrey, Johnson's vice president, on the first ballot. Humphrey had not contested a single primary and was associated with Johnson's Vietnam policy; his nomination further divided the party. When Humphrey narrowly lost the general election to Richard Nixon, insurgent Democrats demanded a change in the nominating process.

The Democratic party, through its McGovern-Fraser Commission, adopted rules designed to make the nominating process more democratic.[8] The commission contended that "popular participation is the way . . . for people committed to orderly political change to fulfill their needs and desires within our traditional political system."[9] Primaries and open party caucuses (meetings open to all rank-and-file party voters who want to attend) were established as the two acceptable methods by which a state could select its delegates to the national convention.

As a consequence, the nominating system in the Democratic party changed from a mixed system of one-third primary states and two-thirds convention states, controlled by party elites, to a reformed system in which nearly three-fourths of the delegates to the national convention were chosen by the voters in primary elections.[10] Many Democratic state legislatures passed primary-election laws, thereby binding Republicans to the change as well.[11]

Serious contenders for nomination would now have to appeal directly to the voters. A Humphrey-type campaign for nomination could no longer hope to succeed. The media's influence correspondingly increased. No amount of backing from party leaders could substitute for support among millions of ordinary people, and if candidates expected to persuade those millions, they had to work through the press.

The press gains more influence in elections

Some analysts have concluded that the McGovern-Fraser reforms did not significantly alter the presidential selection process.[12] They point to the long-term decline of parties, noting that the bosses had nearly disappeared anyway, that several additional states in the 1960s had adopted the primary election as their means of choosing national convention delegates, and that candidates were already increasingly conducting their campaigns through the media, particularly television. This argument has its facts right, but it draws the wrong conclusion. The McGovern-Fraser reforms were significant because they denied party leaders, most of whom were not "bosses" even in the heyday of machine politics, the power to recruit, evaluate, and select party nominees. The reforms meant an end to the party-centered state delegations that were the basis of brokered conventions. In abolishing a deliberative party process, the McGovern-Fraser Commission took control out of the hands of the party regulars and gave it to those presidential hopefuls who were willing to actively campaign for nomination.[13]

The press's restless search for the riveting story works against its intention to provide the voters with a reliable picture of the campaign.

Jimmy Carter's efforts in the year preceding his 1976 presidential nomination exemplified the new reality. Instead of making the traditional rounds among party leaders, Carter traveled about the country meeting with journalists. When the *New York Times*'s R.W. Apple wrote a front-page story about Carter's bright prospects one Sunday in October 1975, his outlook indeed brightened. Other journalists followed with their Carter stories and helped to propel the long-shot Georgian to his party's nomination. Carter would not have won under the old rules.

Of course, the news media's influence in presidential selection had not been inconsequential in earlier times, and in a few instances it had even been crucial. Wendell Willkie was an obscure businessman until the publisher Henry Luce decided that he would make a good president. Luce used his magazines *Time*, *Life*, and *Fortune* to give Willkie the prominence necessary to win the Republican nomination in 1940. By the time of the fall campaign, Luce was providing him with hot speech ideas and meeting with him regularly to plot strategy. Luce complained whenever one of his editors let slip through any comment critical of Willkie. A *Time* reporter wired from the campaign trail: "Take me off this train. All I can do is sit at my typewriter and write, 'Wendell Willkie is a wonderful man. Wendell Willkie is a wonderful man.'"[14]

Nevertheless, the media's role today in helping to establish the election agenda is different from what it was in the past. Once upon a time, the press occasionally played an important part in the nomination of presidential candidates. Now its function is always a key one. The news media do not entirely determine who will win the nomination, but no candidate can succeed without the press. The road to nomination now runs through the newsrooms.

Reform and a new role for the press

Reform Democrats did not take the character of the news media into account when they changed the presidential election process in the early 1970s. Their goal was admirable enough. The system required a change that would give the voters' preferences more weight in the nominating process. But the reformers disregarded the desirability of also creating a process that was deliberative and would allow for the reflective choice of a nominee.

In their determination to abolish the old system, they gave almost no thought to the dynamics of the new one. The McGovern-Fraser Commission's report, *Mandate for Reform*, includes no systematic evaluation of the press's role in the new arrangement. The report had one message: rank-and-file voters would be the kingmakers in the new system.[15]

The claim was naïve. The new structure was plebiscitelike, but much too complex to enable the public to understand its choices without guidance. The system did not pose a yes-no vote on a single issue of policy or leadership. Rather, it asked voters to make a complex decision that is difficult even for seasoned party professionals operating in the context of a deliberative national convention.

The voters would have to receive guidance from somewhere. The real choice the McGovern-Fraser Commission faced in 1970 was not between a system with the party leaders in the middle and one without a mediating agent. In any polity of any size, a complex interaction between the public and its leaders requires an intermediary. Since the press was the only other possible go-between, the McGovern-Fraser Commission selected it without any conscious recognition of having made that choice.

The full significance of the change also escaped the notice of the press. Not a single editorial, analysis piece, or news story about the press's power in the new system appeared in the prestige media when the McGovern-Fraser reforms were adopted.[16] The first campaign under the new system did not alter the situation. In *The Boys on the Bus*, Timothy Crouse described a campaign press corps soured by Vietnam and increasingly adversarial, but otherwise engaged in business as usual.[17]

Nevertheless, the reforms had fundamentally changed the press's role. Its new responsibilities were unlike its duties outside the campaign context and had no exact parallel in elections past.[18]

A constructive role for an adversarial press

The modern campaign requires the press to play a constructive role. When the parties established a nominating process that is essentially a free-for-all between self-generated candidacies, the task of bringing the candidates and voters together in a common effort was superimposed on a media system that was built for other purposes. The press was no longer asked only to keep an eye out for wrongdoing and to provide a conduit for candidates to convey their messages to the voters. It was also expected to guide the voters' decisions. It was obliged to inspect the candidates' platforms, judge their fitness for the nation's highest office, and determine their electability—functions the parties had performed in the past. In addition, the press had to carry out these tasks in a way that would enable the voters to exercise *their* discretion effectively in the choice of nominees.

The columnist Russell Baker hinted at these new responsibilities when he described the press as the "Great Mentioner." The nominating campaign of a candidate who is largely ignored by the media is almost certainly futile, while the campaign of one who receives close attention gets an important boost. In this sense, the press performs the party's traditional role of screening potential nominees for the presidency—deciding which ones are worthy of serious consideration by the electorate and which ones can be dismissed as also-rans. The press also helps to establish the significance of the primaries and caucuses, deciding which ones are critical and how well the candidates must perform in them to be taken seriously.

The press's responsibilities, however, go far beyond news decisions that allocate coverage among the contending contests and candidates. The de facto premise of today's nominating system is that the media will direct the voters toward a clear understanding of what is at stake in choosing one candidate rather than another. Whereas the general election acquires stability from the competition between the parties, the nominating stage is relatively undefined. It features self-starting candidates, all of whom clamor for public attention, each claiming to be the proper representative of his party's legacy and future. It is this confusing situation that the press is expected to clarify.[19]

The press cannot substitute for political institutions

A press-based system seems as if it ought to work. The public gets a nearly firsthand look at the candidates. The alternatives are out in the open for all to see. What could be better?

The belief that the press can substitute for political institutions is widespread. Many journalists, perhaps most of them, assume they can do it effectively.[20] Scholars who study the media also accept the idea that the press can organize elections. Every four years, they suggest that the campaign could be made coherent if the media would only report it differently.[21]

However, the press merely appears to have the capacity to organize the voters' alternatives in a coherent way. The news creates a pseudo-community: citizens feel that they are part of a functioning whole until they try to act upon their news-created awareness. The futility of media-based public opinion was dramatized in the 1976 movie *Network*, when its central character, a television anchorman, becomes enraged at the nation's political leadership and urges his viewers to go to their windows and yell, "I'm mad as hell, and I'm not going to take this anymore!" People heed his instructions, but the chief result of this verbal venting of anger is merely to intensify the public's sense of futility. The press can raise the public's consciousness, but the news itself cannot organize public opinion in any meaningful way.

> *The road to nomination now runs through the newsrooms.*

The press is in the news business, not the business of politics, and because of this, its norms and imperatives are not those required for the effective organization of electoral coalitions and debate. Journalistic values and political values are at odds with each other.

The proper organization of electoral opinion requires an institution with certain characteristics. It must be capable of seeing the larger picture—of looking at the world as a whole and not in small pieces. It must have incentives that cause it to identify and organize those interests that are making demands for policy representation. And it must be accountable for its choices, so that the public can reward it when satisfied and force amendments when dissatisfied.[22]

The press has none of these characteristics. The media has its special strengths, but they do not include these strengths.

The press is a very different kind of organization from the political party, whose role it acquired. A party is driven by the steady force of its traditions and constituent interests, which is why the Democratic leadership in 1952 chose Stevenson, a New Deal liberal, over Kefauver, a border-state populist. The press, in contrast, is "a restless beacon."[23] Its concern is the new, the unusual, and the sensational. Its agenda shifts abruptly when a new development breaks.[24]

The party has the incentive—the possibility of acquiring political power—to give order and voice to society's values. Its raison d'être is to articulate interests and to forge them into a winning coalition. The press has no such incentive and no such purpose. Its objective is the discovery and development of good stories.[25] Television-news executive Richard Salant once said that his reporters covered stories from "nobody's point of view."[26] What he was saying, in effect, was that journalists are driven by news opportunities, not by political values.

The press performs the party's traditional role of screening potential nominees for the presidency.

The press is also not politically accountable. The political party is made accountable by a formal mechanism—elections. The vote gives officeholders a reason to act in the majority's interest, and it offers citizens an opportunity to boot from office anyone they feel has failed them. Thousands of elected officials have lost their jobs this way. The public has no comparable hold on the press. Journalists are neither chosen by the people nor removable by them. Irate citizens may stop watching a news program or buying a newspaper that angers them, but no major daily newspaper or television station has ever gone out of business as a result.

Other democracies have recognized the inappropriateness of press-based elections. Although national voting in all Western democracies is media-centered in the sense that candidates depend primarily on mass communication to reach the voters, no other democracy has a system in which the press fills the role traditionally played by the political party.[27] Journalists in other democracies actively participate in the campaign process, but their efforts take place within an electoral structure built around political institutions. In the United States, however, national elections are referendums in which the candidates stand alone before the electorate and have no choice but to filter their appeals through the lens of the news media.

Notes

1. Walter Lippmann, *Public Opinion* (1922; reprint, New York: Free Press, 1965), p. 229.

2. Carl Bernstein, "It's Press vs. Bush: A Bruising Fight," *Los Angeles Times*, October 25, 1992, p. M1.

3. Lippmann, *Public Opinion*, p. 226.

4. "Clinton's the One," *Media Monitor* (Center for Media and Public Affairs, Washington, D.C.), November 1992, p. 2.

5. Jonathan Alter, "The Smear Heard 'Round the World," *Newsweek*, October 19, 1992, p. 27.

6. Lippmann, *Public Opinion*, p. 229.

7. William R. Keech and Donald R. Matthews, *The Party's Choice* (Washington, D.C.: Brookings Institution, 1976), pp. 103–5.

8. Terry Sanford, *A Danger of Democracy* (Boulder, Co.: Westview Press, 1981), p. 19.

9. Quoted in Austin Ranney, *Participation in American Presidential Nominations 1976* (Washington, D.C.: American Enterprise Institute, 1977), p. 6.

10. The change to a primary-dominated system was not anticipated by the McGovern-Fraser Commission. It assumed that the state parties would merely modify the method of selection they had been using. The smaller number of states that had used the primary method were expected to keep it but to require that the primary vote be binding on delegates. The larger number of states that had relied upon the caucus method were expected simply to open their caucuses to any rank-and-file Democrat who wanted to participate. Unexpectedly, many of the caucus states chose to comply with the rules by switching to the primary-election method of choosing delegates. A basic reason was the judgment of many party regulars that the safest way to comply with the mandated change was to adopt the primary; to retain the open-caucus method (where other party decisions, including the selection of local leaders, could also be made) was to risk a total loss of control of the organization to the insurgents.

11. William Crotty and John S. Jackson III, *Presidential Primaries and Nominations* (Washington, D.C.: American Enterprise Institute, 1977), pp. 44–49.

12. See Howard L. Reiter, *Selecting the President: The Nominating Process in Transition* (Philadelphia: University of Pennsylvania Press, 1985); Richard Rubin, *Press, Party, and President* (New York: Norton, 1981), pp. 147–80.

13. Alan Ehrenhalt, *The United States of Ambition* (New York: Times Books, 1991), p. 265.

14. James David Barber, *The Pulse of Politics: Electing Presidents in the Media Age* (New York: Norton, 1980), pp. 157–58.

15. *Mandate for Reform* (Washington, D.C.: Democratic National Committee, 1970), p. 49.

16. This statement is based on an examination of *New York Times* and *Washington Post* stories at the time the McGovern-Fraser Commission's guidelines were made public.

17. Timothy Crouse, *The Boys on the Bus* (New York: Ballantine, 1974).

18. See Max Kampelman, "The Power of the Press," *Policy Review*, Fall 1978, pp. 11–14.

19. Michael J. Robinson, "Television and American Politics: 1956–1976," in

Reader in Public Opinion and Communication, 3rd ed., ed. Morris Janowitz and Paul Hirsch (New York: Free Press, 1981), p. 109.

20. See "The Press and the Presidential Campaign, 1988," (Seminar proceedings of the American Press Institute, Reston, Va., December 6, 1988).

21. Ibid.

22. See Everett Carll Ladd, *American Political Parties* (New York: Norton, 1970), p. 2.

23. Lippmann, *Public Opinion*, p. 229.

24. Richard Davis, *The Press and American Politics* (New York: Longman, 1992), pp. 21–27.

25. James David Barber, "Characters in the Campaign: The Literary Problem," in *Race for the Presidency*, ed. James David Barber (Englewood Cliffs, N.J.: Prentice-Hall, 1978), pp. 114–17.

26. Quoted in Edward Jay Epstein, *News from Nowhere* (New York: Random House, 1973), p. ix.

27. Holli Semetko, Jay G. Blumler, Michael Gurevitch, and David H. Weaver, with Steve Barkin and G. Cleveland Wilhoit, *The Formation of Campaign Agendas* (Hillsdale, N.J.: Lawrence Erlbaum, 1991), pp. 3, 4.

3

The Media Often Misrepresent Politicians' Messages

James Carville

James Carville, along with Paul Begala, was the political strategist of Bill Clinton's 1992 presidential campaign. He is now a partner in the political consulting firm of Carville and Begala.

The traditional media exercise a great deal of power in electoral politics as a filter of the candidates' messages. The goal of campaign strategists, or "spin doctors," is to get the media to report their candidate's message in the best light. The job of the media, however, is to find new and controversial things to report. Reporters sometimes use shabby techniques to produce controversy in their stories. Moreover, once they write a story, reporters are reluctant to examine it from a different point of view or even to correct errors in it.

No one understands the power of the media in this country. I went into this [1992] campaign believing they were powerful. I didn't know. The power they have is staggering. And they really do guard it.

They like to think of themselves as learned and insightful and thoughtful and considered. They claim the mantle of truth. Hell, truth is they make instant snap judgments and after that all of their time, all of their energy, all of their creativity is spent on nothing but validating their original judgment. Something happens and three minutes after the event they all talk to each other and decide "This is the story," and the story must remain thus in perpetuity. They claim the moral high ground; their job is to report facts and tell people the truth. But information is secondary to them, self-justification is primary. Once the collective media mind is made up, it will not change.

Until you understand that, you can never understand the media. *Their original take is the one that's going to last.* Knowing this, as a political strategist, it is your imperative to get out there right away and make sure your side of the story is the one they see and hear and write and say. That is why you have to be in the first news cycle, not the follow-up; that is why we try everything to get our story out first and best. It's why we went down first in New Hampshire and claimed victory. History gets created in about three minutes. Don't miss it. If you get there a moment too late, you're dead.

Once they've got their story they stick to it. At some point they stop thinking about an issue and just pursue it. There's no one who has dealt with the national media who has not gotten any number of phone calls saying, "I'm writing a story and I want to say this. Can you say it for me?" Reporters try to get you to say what they want you to say, not what you've got to say. If you say what *you* want to say, they keep coming back to try and get you to say what *they* want you to say. I tell them, "Look, we're going to be on this phone an awful long time. Now, do you want me to tell you what I think? Because I'm not going to tell you what you *want* me to think."

"Spin doctors" and Bill Clinton's image

They made up this phrase, "spin doctors." The word "spin," I think, means what political strategists do when we go out and put our candidate in the most favorable light. That's what spin is. Well, la-di-da, guess what? They're right. What do you want me to say? Of course. That's my job. Why don't the media just admit the truth about themselves, that they're way more into self-justification than information? Then we could go on from there.

Take, for example, Bill Clinton. Here was a guy who was my age, who grew up in the South, who cut his teeth on his passion for civil rights and his opposition to the war in Vietnam. And a bunch of Yankee yuppie reporters decided that he was Slick Willie. It's an article of faith among the national media that Bill Clinton was an ambitious politician who tailored his positions to get elected since the doctor slapped him on his butt when he was born.

The word "spin," I think, means what political strategists do when we go out and put our candidate in the most favorable light.

I kept saying, "What are you guys talking about? Do you really think that a guy who was an utterly, totally ambitious political animal would have as his two defining moments entering politics his opposition to the Vietnam war and his passion for civil rights? Look, I'm the same age as him. Do you think that a political consultant, if he was conniving to get his guy governor of Arkansas, would have said, 'What you've got to do is go to Texas and be George McGovern's campaign manager. And you have to take a really strong civil rights stand'? Are you guys nuts?" [Bill Clinton was state coordinator for McGovern's 1972 presidential campaign.]

They would listen to me but they would never accept any evidence to the contrary. They couldn't say, "This is a complex man who has beliefs, and who, like a lot of politicians, is ambitious." If an undeniable fact runs counter to the story they want to write, they will ignore the fact.

They try to be honest people. A lot of them I like. But they're so into self-justification that they have turned journalism into the one institution in America with the least capacity for self-examination and self-criticism. If a political professional criticizes them, they say it's the government that's doing it and hide behind the First Amendment. These people think the First Amendment belongs to them. It doesn't; it belongs to the American people. The ultimate arrogance is that they view any criticism as some sort of censorship or media-bashing. Democrats have Republicans to criticize us; Republicans have Democrats to criticize them. Ford's got GM, GM's got Ford. But the media, they never criticize each other. Thou shalt speak no evil of another reporter.

Reporters' job vs. political strategists' job

There is a natural conflict between reporters and campaign strategists. Reporters, from the day they walk into journalism school, news is defined to them as "something different." Every day the media get up, they're looking for something new and different to report. What campaign strategists are about is focus, repetition, consistency. Every day we get up, we're trying to get them to report the same thing over and over.

So how do we get them to do it?

If you want schoolchildren to eat spinach, you cannot serve them hamburger. If you give them a choice, they ain't going to eat spinach. Now, you can trick them a little bit. You can put some Parmesan cheese on the spinach, you can put on some olive oil, some garlic, you can sauté it, you can add some mushrooms, some hot bacon drippings. But you've got to have spinach. Kids don't like spinach every day. They want cheeseburgers and ice cream, so it's an ongoing struggle.

The media's dietary habits are not particularly healthful. They kind of like their high-fat foods, like cheese fries and patty melts: Gennifer Flowers, Hillary's hairdo. They're not too big on the garden vegetables of the campaign, like job creation and health care costs. And usually, the further down the food chain you go, the worse the dietary habits get. New York tabloids, they like really greasy cheeseburgers, like whether you inhale or not.

> *Our job is to get them to report what we think the campaign message is. Their job is to report what they think is news and controversy.*

Candidates are always asking, "Was the media happy?" Our job is not to make them happy; their job is not to make us happy. Our job is to get them to report what we think the campaign message is. Their job is to report what they think is news and controversy. So we have to make our ideas look controversial. We have to make them look appetizing. We've got to cook this spinach at the right temperature.

I can show you poll after poll that says that people don't vote based solely on the abortion issue. But I guarantee you that for every story out of Washington on education funding there are twenty on abortion funding. Why? Everybody's for education; there's no inherent conflict there. On abortion you've got interest groups on each side, you've got fire, you've got rhetoric. It's a point of conflict. It's cheeseburgers.

Controversies and "equivalency journalism"

I think there are very few dishonest people in the media. Do I think they are out of touch? Yes. Do I think that they love to cover themselves more than they do the candidates? Yes. Do I think that they like to create news where sometimes it doesn't exist? Yes. And do I think that they feed off each other and look at stories in a pack? Yes, I do. But do I think they're bad people? Quite clearly, the answer in almost all instances is no.

One of the shabbiest journalistic techniques that I know of is the man-in-the-street interview. Reporters go out and interview ten people. Do they report back that nine out of ten were for Clinton or for health care or pro-choice? No. They put one person on the air saying one thing and one saying the exact opposite, so they can give equal weight to the positions. In the guise of equal time they have badly skewed what people really think. We call it "equivalency journalism" and it's a very bad trait.

There seems to be more tolerance for sloppiness now than there has been before. If a reporter gets a fact wrong, more often than not he's not even upset. A journalist ought to be outraged by a factual error; it calls into question the profession's entire credibility. At the very least they should say, "I can't believe I did that. I feel terrible." But I've never seen a reporter kick a trash can over the fact that he made an error. Mostly it's "Oh, well, okay, what do you want me to do about it? I'm on deadline. You gonna call my editor and get me in trouble?" I'm not likely to do that, I've got to work with these people. Maybe you get a retraction. But an original error in a page one story isn't properly corrected by a retraction on page A20. Other reporters pick up the incorrect story and it just keeps getting spread over and over again.

The power of CNN television news

The real change in media coverage is the emerging power of CNN. CNN has become a very, very important player in presidential campaigns. *Headline News* as much as anything, but certainly CNN news more than regular network news.

It used to be that the Associated Press had the real effect on campaign coverage. *The New York Times*, *The Washington Post*, and the other majors are all morning papers, while the AP serviced afternoon papers with the first take on breaking campaign events. They were the first story that other people in the media could see.

But there are fewer and fewer afternoon papers in the country, and CNN is on all day, every day. The way the news cycle now works is that you have an event in the morning, the reporters go up to their hotel rooms and are working on their stories from one to two in the afternoon, and they're looking at *Headline News*. It's now becoming an article of faith that television is more important than print, so the first television coverage they see is CNN. If you want to find out what's going on, it's the only game in town during the day. That has an effect. A reporter says, "Well, look, this is what they took out of it. I might have taken something else, but I don't want to be wrong."

According to surveys, CNN does quite well in terms of credibility factor. They don't have a lot of viewers but, hell, as long as you have a hundred reporters looking at you and they are filing stories, you don't need to have numbers to have influence. That influences us. I would say I pay more attention to the CNN people covering us than the amount of viewers would indicate. CNN's influence is definitely growing.

4

Old Media Play a Vital Adversarial Role in Elections

Howard Kurtz

Howard Kurtz is a media analyst and reporter for the Washington Post *newspaper.*

In the 1992 election, voters and politicians turned away from the adversarial, scandal-driven campaign coverage of newspapers—the so-called old media—and shifted to the new media of talk shows and "infomercials" for election news. Ross Perot in particular made effective use of the new media to build a campaign based on opposition to traditional media and politics. But the old media and its attack-dog style played a vital role in exposing the true character of Ross Perot.

By the late spring of 1992 it was clear that the presidential campaign had broken free of the establishment press.

Frustrated by the narrow, cramped agenda of daily journalism, the candidates began to sidestep the national press corps and take their message to a broader audience. If fewer people were reading newspapers and watching the network news, then perhaps they could be reached through Arsenio Hall and Larry King and MTV. If voters were disgusted with the antagonistic queries of Washington reporters, they could ask their own questions on call-in shows and at televised town meetings. The candidates, tired of having their words sliced and diced into a few sentences in the paper, or challenged by the Sunday-morning pontificators, would simply cut out the middleman. All this threatened to make the newspaper reporter obsolete, his narrative function usurped by television, his mediating role awarded to millions of ordinary citizens plugged into 800 numbers.

The New Media vs. the Old Media

It became fashionable to speak of the Old Media (newspaper hacks and starched-shirt talking heads) being eclipsed by the New Media (movies, rap music, talk radio, infotainment shows). The New Media had all the elements that newspapers lacked: passion, excitement, attitude. The new forms spoke to young people who had little interest in bloodless press accounts. They were on the cutting edge with racially and sexually charged messages that only gradually percolated into the headlines. Facts were less important than point of view; Oliver Stone's conspiratorial *JFK*, widely debunked in the mainstream press, was more vivid to many people than the Warren Commission report [on the November 1963 assassination of John F. Kennedy by Lee Harvey Oswald]. The Old Media flacked for a tired establishment; the new version was in touch with "the people." The newspapers that were once the main conveyor belt for news, and the broadcast networks that once commanded mass audiences, now had to compete with hundreds of impudent upstarts.

Tabloid culture and political culture had merged into one great ooze of celebrification.

The idea of using alternative formats to circumvent the national press was not as newfangled as it seemed. FDR gave fireside chats when radio was the hot new medium. Bobby Kennedy appeared with Jack Paar on "The Tonight Show." Richard Nixon tried to soften his image by popping up on "Laugh-In." Jimmy Carter sought regular-guy status by telling *Playboy* he lusted in his heart; Ronald Reagan preached conservatism on Mutual radio; Gary Hart did "Saturday Night Live." That politicians would now rush to appear on the new breed of confessional programs, which catered to movie stars and sex therapists and women who love transvestites, simply underscored how tabloid culture and political culture had merged into one great ooze of celebrification. And the candidates' forays into Oprah-style campaigning were invariably recounted the next day in the newspapers, which were at once mesmerized by their new competitors and resentful at being shoved to the sidelines.

The New Media were particularly important for Bill Clinton as he struggled to reintroduce himself to an electorate that knew him largely as a media caricature. Clinton's negatives were so high after his January 1992 mugging by the press [regarding his relationship with Gennifer Flowers and his draft record] that many pundits pronounced him unelectable. (Fred Barnes wrote a cover story in the *New Republic* [May 4, 1992] titled "Why Clinton Can't Win.") He needed a looser, more relaxed format—broad enough so he could talk about his modest upbringing in rural Arkansas, present his basic message of economic change (which was old news to the campaign reporters) and, yes, even play the saxophone. None of that was possible under the conventions of traditional journalism, which had dismissed the likely Democratic nominee as old news.

The New Media and the rise of Ross Perot

Meanwhile, the spotlight shifted to a man who had seized the possibilities of live television more aggressively than anyone before him. Ross Perot refused to play by the standard rules: He would not subject himself to press conferences or hit the hustings with a planeload of reporters in tow. Instead, he communed with the country from TV studios, reducing political reporters to armchair critics who had to watch him on the tube like everyone else. He was the talk show candidate for president, making his electronic pitch at the elbows of Larry King and Barbara Walters and Katie Couric. He had little use for print journalists, dismissing the Beltway press corps as a relic of old-style politics.

Newspapers "don't matter," Perot insisted, because "what happens on TV is what really impacts on people. I think you could print any story you want on the front page of the *New York Times* and there's no reaction. It just blows away."

Perot seemed far more in touch with the pulse of America than the pack of reporters rushing from one airport to the next. Newspapers religiously chronicled the guests on "Meet the Press," "Face the Nation" and "This Week with David Brinkley," but entertainment shows like "Larry King Live" were off their radar screen. The *consiglieres* of organized journalism paid no attention when Perot told Larry King on February 20 that he would run for president if supporters could get him on all fifty state ballots. It would take a full month before the *Los Angeles Times* and the *Washington Post* gave page-one recognition to the hundreds of thousands of phone calls that were flooding Perot's office. We were not yet tuned into the New Media.

It gradually dawned on reporters that the armies of disaffected Perot volunteers reflected something broader than just a rich gadfly who could bankroll his own challenge. Once the mainstream media had certified Perot as a genuine phenomenon, he was buoyed by a gusher of fawning coverage. The infatuation stage had begun. Perot was Mr. None of the Above, thumbing his nose at a bankrupt political system and an arrogant press corps that seemed to embody its values.

"The elfin, crewcut Texas billionaire is poised to cast himself as a kind of Lone Ranger from the Lone Star State ready to ride into Washington to clean up the mess," the *New York Times* observed.

"Computer tycoon, business reformer and unabashed patriot . . . a billionaire entrepreneur who has spawned a folklore of almost mythic proportions . . . perhaps the greatest threat to the political establishment in a generation," proclaimed the *Wall Street Journal*.

The effusive prose masked a growing indignation among reporters that this Dallas maverick could soar in the polls without getting down in the trenches with them. He was, the *Boston Globe* sniffed, "a crewcut billionaire who sounds more like a cow town sheriff than a world leader." Perot was running on platitudes, promising to wipe out the budget deficit "without breaking a sweat," an absurd claim he had no intention of clarifying. Yet voters loved the way he brushed off reporters like nettlesome gnats. It was like the White House press corps trying to nail Ronald Reagan for stretching the truth; Perot seemed to stand for something, and many people simply didn't care whether he met some journalistic threshold for specificity.

The Old Media vs. Perot

The press turned on Perot in a few short weeks, telescoping the normal process as if to compensate for his avoidance of the primary election gauntlet. Soon the *New York Times*, *Wall Street Journal*, *Washington Post*, *Los Angeles Times*, Associated Press and *Dallas Morning News*, his hometown paper, were giving Perot the flyspeck treatment: He had won a special tax break by donating $55,000 to members of the House Ways and Means Committee. He had convinced the government to invest in a Fort Worth, Texas, airport near land his family owned. He had received special favors from the Nixon White House and had discussed spending $50 million—perhaps to buy the *Washington Star* or ABC—on a PR campaign to burnish Nixon's image. His computer firm, Electronic Data Systems, had fired people for wearing beards or committing adultery. He had discussed business opportunities with Vietnamese officials during his much-ballyhooed mission to find missing American servicemen [in December 1969]. He had hired private detectives to investigate employees and rivals. Despite his stance against raising taxes, he had written in the *Washington Post* in 1987: "We must cut spending and raise taxes to pay our bills. We all know it."

Some columnists—the *Times'* William Safire, the *Post'*s Richard Cohen—began crusading against Perot. The press dug up almost daily examples of his weird behavior. In 1955 Perot had sought an early release from the Navy, calling it "a fairly Godless organization" where he had to endure the spectacle of sailors drinking and cursing like, well, sailors. Richard Connor, publisher of the *Fort Worth Star-Telegram*, recalled how Perot, upset about coverage of his son's business dealings, had warned that he had photographs to prove that one of Connor's employees was having an affair with a city official.

David Remnick, then a *Washington Post* reporter, offered a similarly strange tale. During a routine interview, Perot had opened his office safe and produced a photograph of a top Pentagon official, Richard Armitage, and a young Asian woman that he said "completely compromised" Armitage.

Yet Ross Perot was soaring above the reach of the Old Media. He often denounced his press critics in personal terms. When asked about a 1988 column by Laura Miller of the *Dallas Times Herald*, reporting that he had called for house-to-house searches in the war on drugs, Perot accused her of "flights of fantasy." When Linda Wertheimer of National Public Radio pressed him on the air about his failed effort to rescue a New York brokerage firm in the 1970s, Perot accused her of a "classic setup . . . and I'm sure you had a smirk on your mouth as you got me into this." Perot insisted that hostile interviews worked to his advantage by making voters angry, and perhaps he was right: By mid-May he had passed both Bush and Clinton in the polls.

"This country does have a weird fixation on the businessman/savior," columnist Jack Newfield wrote. "Remember, four years ago people were talking about Donald Trump running for president."

Voter disgust with the Old Media

As spring turned into summer, the prospect that Perot might actually become president was unnerving to many reporters, who interviewed his volunteers as if they were strange fanatics. What they found were ordinary, middle-class folks disgusted with the kind of slash-and-burn politics the press specialized in covering.

"Are Perot's supporters on a dangerous flight from reality?" Don

Kimelman asked in the *Philadelphia Inquirer.* "Or, worse yet, are they crypto-fascists looking for a führer who will end the political deadlock that our messy democracy has produced? Hardly. . . . They are, for the most part . . . decent, levelheaded people." *Boston Globe* columnist Derrick Jackson, however, was more dismissive: "Millions of blind mice are running into Ross Perot's cage. Stupid little creatures they are."

Millions of people had become disconnected from the kind of poll-driven, battering-ram politics chronicled by the Old Media.

Perot's rivals quickly followed him onto the talk show circuit, hoping for a whiff of his magic formula. Clinton jammed for Arsenio, did breakfast on "Good Morning America" and rapped with young folks on MTV. Bush fielded questions on "20/20" and "CBS This Morning." The candidates got hours and hours of free airtime and relished the chance to make their case, unedited and unfiltered. They got plenty of softballs they could knock out of the park, and without the adversarial follow-up that had become a journalistic trademark. As a bonus, they could reach younger, more alienated viewers who had little use for newspapers.

On a deeper level, the talk show campaign was a rejection of the prosecutorial culture of the national press that had reached its apogee with Watergate. It was, at bottom, a healthy development. Millions of people had become disconnected from the kind of poll-driven, battering-ram politics chronicled by the Old Media. If professional reporters were more persistent than Aunt Millie from Omaha calling in from her kitchen, they were frequently less substantive and more concerned with strategy and inside baseball. When Bush held a prime-time news conference on June 4 (which the Big Three networks pointedly refused to broadcast), nearly half the questions were about Perot, the polls and other horse-race matters. Some were downright inane; a *USA Today* reporter asked what Bush would say to Perot if he ran into him on the street. It was yet another reminder of why people were tuning us out.

The Old Media investigate Perot's character

In his disdain for details, however, Perot had underestimated the ability of newspapers to set the campaign agenda, even in the television age. His dealings with one rather famous reporter were about to come back to haunt him. During the 1988 campaign, Perot had gathered a wealth of documents and allegations about George Bush and passed them to Bob Woodward. The *Washington Post* sleuth was investigating the then vice president, and Perot, who detested Bush, was only too eager to help.

Perot told Woodward he had looked into a controversial Texas land deal that might bear Bush's fingerprints. Woodward and a colleague, Walter Pincus, say they spoke to the billionaire on "background," meaning they could use the information but could not attribute it to him (Perot recalls the discussions as being totally off the record). Perot described the situation as a "mini–Teapot Dome" [referring to the scandal of the 1920s] and gave the reporters two vinyl binders full of documents.

Perot offered to obtain the records on two of Bush's Texas invest-ments and later sent them to the reporters. He dropped other tantalizing leads, recalling how he had once warned Bush that two of his sons were associating with unsavory characters.

The leads went nowhere, and the *Post* never published Perot's mater-ial. Four years later, however, Perot's Watergate-style penchant for inves-tigating his enemies had become big news. Woodward faced a thorny dilemma: Perot had been a confidential source, yet the very transaction for which Woodward had promised him anonymity was now part of the hottest story in town.

Those annoying Old Media reporters had been right to press Perot about the issues he so calmly finessed at Larry King's elbow.

Woodward called Perot. "I've got to write about you as an investiga-tor," he said.

"I don't want any of that out," Perot replied, saying it would distract from the real issues of the campaign.

"The situation's changed," Woodward said. "I've got an obligation. I'm going to write about it in some form. You're running for president and it describes who you are."

Perot refused to put their conversations on the record. Woodward told James Squires, the former *Chicago Tribune* editor acting as Perot's spokesman, that he was going with the story. Squires left a message con-firming that Perot had passed information on the Texas land deal to the *Post*, but he disputes Woodward's contention that this amounted to putting it on the record. As for the other "background" material, Wood-ward and his coauthor, John Mintz, artfully worded their article so that they never said exactly where the stuff was coming from, although read-ers could infer that Perot was the source.

Defending the story on Perot

The *Post*'s banner story on June 21 caused a sensation. The image of In-spector Perot, private eye, took hold in the popular culture. The electronic town hall candidate reacted like an old-style pol: He summoned David Broder, dean of the political press corps, for an interview. Perot told the *Post* columnist that the recent spate of negative stories were the product of "Republican dirty tricks." (This was demonstrably false in the case of the *Post* story, which had obviously come from Perot's own lips.) After weeks of ignoring reporters at his rallies, Perot called his first news con-ference to defend himself.

The talk around Washington was whether Woodward, who was still protecting Deep Throat twenty years after Watergate, had burned his source. Bill Safire charged that the *Post* had been a "patsy" for Perot and that Woodward had "confessed" to the secret dealings for fear of being ex-posed. Once again, I had no choice but to do a story about my own paper.

Woodward told me he had been "very aggressive" with Perot, but said he had "other sources" for much of the information and that "the ground rules were strictly observed. . . . I feel absolutely comfortable." But Squires suggested that Woodward had violated his confidentiality pledge. "One of the most famous reporters in the country, doer of good deeds, pursuer of sin and corruption in high places, is calling Perot, working on a Bush investigation," he said. "It's Woodward who was investigating Bush. Perot gives Woodward what he asked for. That act, right there, turns into Perot 'investigating' Bush and Bush's children."

The *Post* compounded the problem by not being straightforward about the origins of the story. We were pointing the finger at Perot for investigating Bush when the paper had been a willing accomplice. And while there is a difference between a newspaper and a private businessman conducting such inquiries, we failed to make that argument by fudging the facts.

Unfortunately, a *Post* editor killed my explanatory piece after the first edition, ostensibly to make room for late-breaking news but creating the perception that the paper had something to hide. I complained to Len Downie that we still had not adequately explained how the Woodward story got into print, and he agreed to let me write a longer piece about the controversy, which ran two days later.

Attack-dog journalism does its job

Other newspapers, meanwhile, were pummeling Perot regularly, with television following suit. The attack-dog stage had arrived. Perot started sinking in the polls. He tried to explain away his comment that he wouldn't have homosexuals in his Cabinet. He addressed an NAACP audience as "you people." Days later, on July 16, Perot pulled the plug on his candidacy.

The newspaper reporters that Perot so casually scorned had helped blow him out of the race. It was done like "a Mafia hit, with smooth professionalism," Richard Cohen said admiringly. Perot had a fine time running against the press, but when the press started hitting back, he quickly folded his cards. He couldn't take the heat, couldn't abide having snotty reporters challenge the mythologized version of his life story and point an accusatory finger each time he lied. It was journalism at its best, for the searing spotlight of press scrutiny essentially exposed this billionaire populist as a paper tiger.

Some publications clearly enjoyed kicking the Texan while he was down. "The Quitter," said *Newsweek*'s cover. "WHAT A WIMP!" declared the *New York Post*. The *Kansas City Star* called him a "fraud," the *Miami Herald* a "chicken." The man who declared every problem "pretty simple," who said he could easily eliminate the deficit, belatedly embraced a plan to raise taxes and cut Social Security and other entitlement programs. It was a tacit acknowledgment that his no-sweat assurances had been wrong all along.

It turned out that those annoying Old Media reporters had been right to press Perot about the issues he so calmly finessed at Larry King's elbow. Ross Perot had bowed out in large measure because he could not stomach the daily combat with the press and that spoke volumes about his unsuitability for the Oval Office.

5

New Media Connect Politicians with Voters

Dee Dee Myers

Dee Dee Myers served as press secretary for the 1992 Clinton campaign and as White House press secretary. She is currently the cohost (with Mary Matalin) of the cable television talk show Equal Time.

In the 1992 election, the Clinton campaign made successful use of new technologies to reach voters with its message. Voters, in turn, were able to use these technologies to voice their problems and ideas to the candidate. Bill Clinton was elected because he offered the nation a better vision, but his effective use of alternative media—such as talk shows, electronic mail, and faxes—to communicate that vision put him in touch with voters and their concerns and gave him the margin of victory.

In 1992, the American people voted to "throw the bums out." Fed up with a government they believed was more interested in protecting special interests than in promoting the public interest, they went to the polls in record numbers and voted for change. The American people were alienated, disenfranchised, and certain that four more years of "business as usual" would send the country even further down the road to ruin.

A number of factors—from a stubborn recession and persistently high unemployment to the emergence of Ross Perot—combined to unleash this demand for change. Ultimately, Bill Clinton's vision of economic change and national revitalization provided a renewed spirit for the nation and sealed his victory.

Technological advancement and political change

Although there will never be a substitute for the charisma of a candidate or the strength of a message, the modes and methods of communication can play a major role in the outcome of an election. The presidential campaign signaled a dramatic change in the strategy of political communication. The methods became part of the message. The new approach was inspired, in part, by a political imperative of reconnecting alienated voters

Dee Dee Myers, "New Technology and the 1992 Clinton Presidential Campaign," *American Behavioral Scientist*, vol. 37, no. 2 (November 1993), pp. 181–87; ©1993 by Sage Publications, Inc. Reprinted by permission of Sage Publications, Inc.

to the process of electing a new president. It was made possible by technological changes almost unimaginable a generation ago.

The Clinton communication strategy recognized that the basic, fundamental character of "news" had changed. Technological advances have led to an explosion in the number of news outlets available to distribute information. Where people once obtained most of their information from daily newspapers and the 6 p.m. network news, CNN brings events from Milwaukee to Mogadishu into America's living rooms 24 hours a day. In addition, local television and radio stations, small-town newspapers, and on-line computer services cover everything from PTA meetings to global summits. They have become an almost unlimited source of opportunities for creative campaigns.

In campaigns past, an allegation made against a candidate one day was often answered the next. But today, through the proliferation of computer modems, faxes, E-mail, interactive satellites, and other new modes of communication, several rounds of charges and countercharges are often exchanged in time for the evening news. In short, the news cycle has contracted; the charge-response that used to take a couple of days now takes a couple of hours. A quick response can turn a negative for one candidate into a negative for another. In the words of legendary campaign strategist James Carville, "Speed kills."

These changes have profound implications for political campaigns. Clinton's strategists recognized this and made a conscious decision to adapt the campaign to the new environment. Thus the "war room" was born. The emphasis on taking advantage of technology to monitor and ultimately shape the news helped us accomplish at least five tactical and strategic goals.

Campaign strategy and new technology

First, the campaign developed a strategy of rapid response around a "get hit—hit back harder" philosophy. The war room became the 24-hour hub of the campaign, constantly monitoring the newswires, talk radio, and CNN, as well as movements and schedules of the opposition. From President Bush, Vice President Quayle, and cabinet members to most Republican surrogates, this constant monitoring of breaking news, surrogate attacks, and opposition research provided the decision makers with the information to readily and rapidly respond to any attacks. No charge went unnoticed; no attack went unanswered.

An illustration of the rapid response came the night President Bush gave his acceptance speech at the Republican National Convention in Houston, Texas. Our opposition research team obtained an advance copy of his remarks, and the war room was able to recast its contents into a "reality versus rhetoric" document. We took what President Bush said and refuted it with hard numbers. This analysis was produced so quickly that major TV networks used it as the counterpoint in their live postspeech commentary. At one point, CNN's Charles Bierbauer could be seen standing on the convention floor, waving a faxed copy of our document.

Second, we reinforced a targeted political strategy with a targeted communication strategy, using specific news outlets to reach specific audiences. The campaign identified 18 targeted states and set an aggressive, daily presence in each. Technology—including satellite links, faxes, and radio feeds—was used to serve interested markets by highlighting specialized issues.

In conjunction with local and state organizations, the Clinton/Gore field operation successfully created news in local markets that reinforced the national message. The best examples of national campaign interaction with grassroots organizations took place during the bus tours. These trips not only allowed the campaign to earn free media coverage on a national level but, more important, allowed us to dominate media coverage on a local level. The communications department would "manifest" local media on the buses, giving them affordable access to the campaign trail. The opportunity for "locals" to cover the campaign for an extended period of time generated extensive positive coverage and gave the communities a sense of excitement and participation.

The presidential campaign signaled a dramatic change in the strategy of political communication. The methods became part of the message.

Third, using interactive satellite, telephone technology, and electronic computer communications, we were able to put the candidate in more than one place at one time. The campaign was successful in reaching a broader audience by using technology to do regional interviews, beam the candidate into meetings and gatherings in other cities, and transmit speeches and press releases electronically.

In Governor Clinton's campaign, these new ways of communicating served two basic functions. They allowed our message to reach an extraordinary number of voters who might not otherwise hear it, and they empowered countless individuals with the ability to participate directly in the political dialogue.

One little-noticed development that illustrates the interactive nature of modern technology is the use of electronic mail. During the general election campaign, the text of all Bill Clinton's speeches as well as his daily schedule, press releases, and position papers were made available through on-line computer services, such as Compuserve and Prodigy. For the first time, ordinary citizens had an easy way to obtain information that was previously available only to the national press corps. Instead of seeing an 8-second sound bite chosen by a network producer, voters could read an entire speech. This inventive technology has already become a new medium of communication: *Time* magazine recently announced that it will become available on electronic bulletin boards, allowing readers to contact editors via computer modem.

Fourth, we were able to paint a more complete picture of the candidate by using varied and longer-format media opportunities. We believed that the more people saw and heard Bill Clinton, the more likely they were to support him. Thus the best opportunities were extended formats, such as town hall meetings, *Larry King Live, Arsenio,* and radio talk shows, like Don Imus' in New York City [*Imus in the Morning*].

The campaign used this format extensively. Beginning in the New

Hampshire primary, the Clinton campaign used the town hall format as an opportunity to put the candidate in a natural setting to address voters and their concerns directly. This worked for several reasons. First, voters most often asked about the "pocketbook" issues that Clinton was espousing, such as health care reform, job development, and income growth. Thus the campaign was able to steer the political debate away from distracting process issues and refocus the discussion on the economy. Second, we were able to showcase Bill Clinton's impressive breadth of knowledge and personal warmth. Finally, less traditional settings, such as the MTV and Nashville Network interviews, showed Governor Clinton as an innovative leader willing to appear in nontraditional forums.

The fifth strategic accomplishment of the 1992 campaign was the combining of new technologies with the use of surrogate speakers. Whether it was reinforcing the candidate's message or responding to attacks, the Clinton campaign reached very specific audiences with the use of its surrogates. Al Gore and Hillary Rodham Clinton were the primary spokespersons for the campaign, but we also used less prominent surrogates with regional or issue appeal. For example, Boston Mayor Ray Flynn conducted satellite interviews in such key markets as Michigan and Pennsylvania, where he had a strong following among organized labor.

Our coordinated surrogate operations worked especially well in the presidential debates. Plugging into both satellites and radio, the surrogate strategy used as many as two dozen officials—from James Carville to Admiral William Crowe—to amplify the campaign's message to multiple audiences in targeted markets.

Reaching more voters

The surrogate operation, and the campaign's communication strategy as a whole forever changed the methods and tactics of disseminating a candidate's political message. However, Bill Clinton's victory was not primarily one of technology or tactics. The bottom line on the '92 campaign is that Bill Clinton won the election because he offered the nation a vision of economic revitalization and collective hope for a better future.

Nonetheless, communication devices played an integral and interesting role. High technology allowed our message to reach an extraordinary number of voters who might not otherwise have heard it and empowered countless individuals to participate in the political dialogue. Achieving these goals was one of our campaign's proudest communications achievements, one which sets a model for future campaigns.

High-tech communications grew to be more than just a way of delivering the message; it became part of the message. The reconnection of leaders with the people and the drawing of the nation closer to political ideas are the lasting legacies of the '92 campaign. As new technologies continue to shape communication, flexibility and innovation will continue to provide the margin of victory.

6

Alternative Media Encourage Voter Participation

Larry King

Larry King has hosted Larry King Live *on CNN since 1985 and other television and radio talk shows since 1956. He is also the author of a number of autobiographical books.*

During the 1992 election campaign, voters were angered because they felt that politicians and the traditional media were out of touch with the everyday concerns of regular people. Alternative media, such as talk shows, offered voters and politicians a way to communicate with each other. Talk shows are a healthy supplement to the regular media in elections because they discourage negative campaigning, encourage voter participation, and develop voter interest in politics and candidates.

The 1992 campaign was the first time I can remember there being more interest in an election at the end of the process than at the beginning. At the start of the campaign Bush seemed unbeatable. In the final weeks he seemed unelectable. Ross Perot had reentered the race, capturing many of the moderate voters who might have helped the president come from behind. Perot stripped some support from Clinton, too, and the polls were narrowing. But the Arkansas governor fought hard to maintain his lead. He was "robo-candidate," campaigning virtually nonstop from town to town, talk show to talk show.

Larger television audiences and a higher voter turnout

Huge audiences—more than eighty million viewers—tuned in for each of the presidential and vice presidential debates. Millions of viewers also watched Perot's paid, half-hour "infomercials." And the ratings were unusually high whenever a candidate appeared on television for an interview or call-in session. At "Larry King Live" our ratings for candidate appearances rivaled our audiences during the 1991 Persian Gulf War, when much of the world was glued to CNN. The campaign became a sort of miniseries—perhaps as big as "Roots" in 1977 or "The Thorn Birds" in

1983. Viewers tuned in nightly to find out what was going to happen to Bill, George, and Ross. We were all on a first-name basis by then. We knew them that well.

More than 104 million Americans voted in the 1992 presidential election, the largest turnout ever. That was up 14 percent from 91.6 million voters in 1988—the biggest increase in forty years. It was also the highest percentage turnout among eligible voters since the Kennedy-Nixon race in 1960. Exit polls showed that 11 percent of those voting were pulling the lever in an election for the first time. And if anyone doubts their impact, consider this: just under half of these first-time voters—about 5.5 million people—supported Clinton. That accounted for nearly all of Clinton's 5.8 million vote margin.[1]

In 1992 political alienation turned into frustration. And the high voter turnout was a by-product of the same anger that made talk shows so important that year. The public was angry about gridlock in Washington, about a government that seemed unable or unwilling to address mounting problems. They were nervous about the economy. The recession may not have been as deep or difficult as many others since World War II, as the Bush campaign tried vainly to remind voters. But economic uncertainty was more intense than ever. People were tired of election-year promises candidates never intended to keep. And they were fed up with politicians who thought meeting with contributors was more important than meeting with constituents.

In speeches during the Democratic primaries, Jerry Brown often asked his audience to raise their hands if they had ever given a political candidate at least one thousand dollars. Few people ever had. No one here has given that much money, Brown would say, but the people who have are the ones who really run the government. It was one of Brown's best bits. By tapping this anti-Washington sentiment—with populist rhetoric, his 800 number, and a self-imposed one hundred dollar limit on campaign contributions—Brown kept his candidacy alive longer than any of Clinton's other rivals in the primaries.

Much of the public felt the country was being run by a small group of people living comfortably under a bubble on the banks of the Potomac. And the press, for the most part, seemed locked under that dome, too. The voices outside were muffled, inaudible. Talk shows were like a glass cutter, a way for the public to reach the people under the bubble.

Talk shows empower people

For most people, of course, this was a vicarious process. Millions of people watched the candidates on "Larry King Live" in 1992, but only about ten dozen actually reached the presidential and vice presidential contenders on our show. In a July 1993 poll by the Times Mirror Center, only 11 percent of those surveyed said they had ever called a talk show, and only 6 percent of the respondents said they had ever talked on the air.[2]

But people did not have to pick up the phone themselves to feel empowered. Just seeing the telephone number on their TV screens or hearing it on their radios, knowing they could call if they wanted to, hearing other people voice their own fears and frustrations was liberating enough.

The people who do call in to talk shows are more frustrated with government and the status quo than society on the whole, as the Times Mirror Center poll suggests. But they are still able spokesmen and spokeswomen for widespread public sentiment. And, for a candidate or office holder, understanding their feelings is good politics. Mario Cuomo says, "If the voice you hear on the call-in show is more emphatically negative than the public at large, okay. But still you come away with a distinct feeling that there are a lot of people, even if they're not 51 percent, who are very unhappy. And that's significant, and the reason for their unhappiness is significant, whether you think they're right or wrong."[3]

Talk shows also showed the public that *they* were responsible for many of the nation's problems, as Perot repeatedly reminded audiences during his campaign. "Who's at fault?" he asked rhetorically during a March 1992 speech at Washington's National Press Club. "First thing you've got to do in our country is blame somebody, right? Well, go home tonight and look in the mirror. . . . You and I are at fault because we own this country, and there is the problem in a nutshell. We've abdicated our ownership responsibilities."[4]

> *The high voter turnout was a by-product of the same anger that made talk shows so important [in 1992].*

In many ways talk shows were the mirror Perot spoke of. Gridlock begins at home, as our callers often proved. They would phone in to complain about how wasteful and undisciplined the government was. Cut spending! Balance the budget! But any ideas for doing either provoked just as many complaints. Don't cut my benefits! Don't close my local military base or slash funding for my pet project! And don't you dare raise my taxes! Damned if you do, and damned if you don't. No wonder Washington seemed to be spinning its wheels.

Among Clinton's budget-cutting ideas, for instance, was a proposal to reduce administrative overhead for federally sponsored university research. But even this modest idea provoked a typical call from a concerned research administrator from Yale when Clinton was on our show in early October. "I wonder if you realize what the implications are to the continuation of medical research in the country if you're successful in saving almost a billion dollars on university research," the caller said. "Also, the implications to people's jobs—namely, mine."[5]

Clinton said that by cutting administrative costs, he hoped to free more funds for actual research. I'm sure that was little consolation to the administrator, who was understandably preoccupied with his own livelihood. But voters generally began to recognize that they would have to straighten themselves out and agree to sacrifice if they really wanted the government to straighten itself out. That message fueled the Perot movement, as it had Paul Tsongas's candidacy in the Democratic primaries. It rang true even among those who would never vote for Perot. There were plenty of people who thought Perot did not have the answers. But no one asked the questions better than he did.

Perot told voters they had to take back the political process—from special interests, from the press. And call-in programs gave them a tool with which to do it. Talk shows meant anyone with a phone had the sort of direct access to candidates they thought only lobbyists could buy. They asked the questions. They set the agenda.

"Voters wanted to hear from the candidates themselves," Clinton strategist James Carville says. They wanted "to know what so-and-so is saying, not what somebody said they were saying. . . . Talk shows offered that."[6]

Talks shows encourage positive campaigning

Talk shows also offered the candidates more than the nine seconds they typically got each night on the news to make their case. A candidate could ramble at length on any subject. And because their positions did not have to be explained in less than a third of the time of your average beer commercial, candidates could afford to take risks. They could take difficult stands, unpopular positions, knowing that they would have time to explain themselves. Clinton could talk about raising taxes. Perot could talk about cutting popular programs. And Bush could try to explain why the economy was not in as bad shape as much of the public thought it was.

Talk shows were also an alternative to the thirty-second attacks that dominate political advertising. The increasing nastiness of campaigns was a major factor in the public's rejection of the political system before 1992. Negative campaigning actually discourages participation by giving people reasons not to vote for a particular candidate. It is much easier to convince people not to vote for someone than it is to get them to switch their vote. So, in the cynical mathematics of political mud-wrestling, if I convince more of your voters to stay home than you do mine, I win.

These tactics fall flat on talk shows. Callers and viewers want to know why they should vote *for* you, not why they shouldn't vote for your opponent. When Quayle came on our show in July, a week after the Democratic National Convention, he was predictably critical of Clinton and Gore and promised to focus on their "vulnerabilities." He talked about "family values." He talked about Clinton's plans to raise taxes. "I'm . . . going to tell the truth about Bill Clinton and Al Gore," he promised. "They don't like being called liberal, but they are liberal."

Our first caller that night was not impressed. "I see that you all are focusing on Mr. Clinton's and Mr. Gore's campaign . . . ," he said to the vice president. "When are you going to get off their campaign and talk about what [you are] going to do to make the country better?"

Quayle answered by briefly summing up Bush's economic proposals, but then turned back to the Democratic ticket. "You've got to remind people . . . what Bill Clinton and Al Gore are all about," Quayle said. "They come out of New York City and they say, 'We are these raging moderates.' That is a bunch of hooey. You know, Al Gore's voting record is the same as Ted Kennedy. Now, is Ted Kennedy a moderate? No. Bill Clinton as governor of Arkansas . . . [raised] taxes something like 128 different times. His record down there is not a record of moderation. . . . This is a trick. I mean, it was a slick convention, and I congratulate them for it. . . . But they are trying to paint themselves as moderates, and they are not moderates. They may be able to fool the people of New York City, but they cannot be allowed to fool the American people."[7]

In one tirade Quayle craftily conjured up several of the Republicans' favorite bogeymen: liberals, Ted Kennedy, taxes, even New York City. But in doing so he seemed to prove the caller's point. Quayle was better at explaining what was wrong with the Democratic nominees than what was good about the Republican administration. Our audience seemed to want something more.

Talk shows vs. traditional media campaign formats

But talk shows did not just serve the public. Carville says the "alternative" media were good hunting grounds for candidates seeking support. The audiences who tuned in to the traditional outlets for political news, such as the networks' Sunday morning interview shows, were mostly "people who are pretty interested in public affairs and [who] don't tend to be very undecided," he says.[8] In other words, Clinton would have a better chance of reaching the people he needed to reach—people who might vote for him, not people who already knew they would or who knew they wouldn't—on "Larry King Live" or the "Arsenio Hall Show" than on "Meet the Press."

Talk shows meant anyone with a phone had the sort of direct access to candidates they thought only lobbyists could buy.

Candidates do have to be careful and selective in their use of alternative media. A member of the cast of "Saturday Night Live" once asked Paul Tsongas if he would consider hosting the show. After a few days Tsongas decided this informal invitation was not in his best interests as a candidate. "I was trying to present myself as a serious truth teller," he says. But it was a tough decision. "It's funny," he says. "I'm in the middle of a campaign, and all I'm thinking about is my opening monologue. . . . And it was difficult to say no because I'd already developed the monologue, and I thought it was pretty funny."[9]

Mandy Grunwald, the media consultant who proposed that Clinton appear on "Arsenio Hall," says she would not be surprised if a candidate "self-destructs" in 1996 trying to repeat the Arkansas governor's late-night coup. "Often what happens is people repeat the tactical success of past campaigns instead of understanding the strategic imperative for them . . . ," she explains. "We needed to explain to people who Bill Clinton was, what his life was about, what he was about, what he was about in personal terms. We had a strategic mandate to do that."[10] And Clinton was charming enough to pull it off. Another candidate in another circumstance might look foolish.

Generally speaking, though, the rise of talk shows and other unconventional media outlets for political information is good for the process, and even good for the traditional press, because it creates more interest in the candidates and the issues. Viewers who see Clinton on "Arsenio Hall" are unlikely to cast their vote simply because they think he plays a mean sax. But by playing the saxophone he may interest those viewers enough to want to find out more about his candidacy. The same was true for call-in shows.

"My selfish view on all this is that the more people get exposed to politics and hooked on it, then the more likely they'll be to gravitate towards 'Meet the Press' . . . and the more traditional programs," Tim Russert [host of NBC's "Meet the Press"] says, adding that his show's ratings went up "considerably" during the 1992 campaign. "We were the beneficiary, I believe, of a lot of people who were pulled into the process who normally wouldn't have been exposed to it. But they watch 'Larry King' on a nightly basis, they watch all the Hollywood stars and all the other people that [go on] that program, and they get hooked on the politics, too. Maybe it was just a spectator sport . . . but it is not something that is going to be hurtful."[11]

Talk shows and scandals

Candidates' extended exposure to the audience on call-in shows also helped voters make judgments about them as people. The conversational setting is different from the confrontational approach of some journalistic programs. On talk shows politicians can relax and act like living, breathing human beings, instead of scarred and callous pols going into battle. Both approaches have their merits. And, as a candidate appears repeatedly in both formats, his or her constituents can develop a rounded impression. "The longer [a] person is in your living room," Gary Hart says, the more you can decide for yourself whether he or she makes any sense, is telling the truth, is of sound character, and all the qualities you want for national leadership."[12]

Such an opportunity might have helped Hart in May 1987, when he withdrew from the Democratic presidential primaries amid press questions about his private life. The *Miami Herald* had reported that the former Colorado senator spent a weekend with model Donna Rice in his Washington town house, and other news organizations were also pursuing rumors about his extramarital activities. Some in Hart's campaign proposed buying a block of television time for Hart to tell his side of the story, but he decided against it and ended his candidacy.

The rise of talk shows and other unconventional outlets for political information is good for the process . . . because it creates more interest in the candidates and the issues.

Could Hart have remained a candidate and used talk shows to bypass scandal-hungry reporters? He doesn't think so. "There was too much chaos then . . . ," he says. "It was made clear to me that it was not going to end. It wasn't one incident that made my decision. It was the clear signal from portions of the media that they were just not going to let up. . . . If I'd been Perot, I could have bought all the [air] time in the world and they still wouldn't have left me alone. . . . There was no way out of it."[13]

I'm not so sure. The public is more forgiving than many politicians think. Admission—even partial admission—works, as Clinton showed when he was asked "Gary Hart" questions in 1992, or as Richard Nixon showed me during a January 1992 interview.

"Is it hard to come back to this city?" I asked the former president. "Is it hard to drive by the Watergate?"

"Well, I've never been in the Watergate," Nixon said.

"Never been in?"

"No," he said. "Other people were in there, though—unfortunately."[14] That regret, that self-deprecating humor, was very disarming.

The conversational tone of a talk show and its humanizing effect are perfectly suited for a politician who is in trouble. John Sununu had to resign as Bush's White House chief of staff in 1991 after he was repeatedly skewered in the press for abusing White House travel perks. The day Sununu resigned he was on the road with Bush. He called me from *Air Force One* to ask if he could come on the show that night and tell his side of the story. "I wanted to explain [the resignation] directly to people rather than let it get translated" through the press, he said.[15]

Talk shows and "softball" questions

The chance to communicate directly, unfiltered by the press, is talk TV's biggest draw for politicians. Perot says that live, unedited programs "allow a person to say what he or she wants to say in their own words without having it rephrased. Then the viewer, I think, without any question feels that they're getting it straight. . . . My favorite expression [in edited interviews] has been that my answer would be printed correctly, but they would change the question."[16]

The chance to communicate directly, unfiltered by the press, is talk TV's biggest draw for politicians.

Some talk show critics miss the filter. They say callers often ask "softball" questions. But Perot knows better than most how tough audiences can be on a candidate. On NBC's "Today" show, he answered a call from "Roberta" in Vero Beach, Florida, who wanted to know if Perot planned to eliminate Social Security benefits for those earning more than sixty thousand dollars a year.

Perot said that wealthy Americans had to sacrifice to preserve the American dream. "Like when you and I were young, in the [Great] Depression, things were very bad," he said. "But we had a dream, and it's best expressed . . . in the song from [the musical] Annie." Perot then launched into a chorus of "Tomorrow." "Isn't it sad now [that] your grandchildren, my grandchildren, are wondering if they will have the American dream, too?"

"Today" cohost Katie Couric asked Roberta if she was satisfied with Perot's answer.

"Well," Roberta said, "he didn't really answer the question."

"Well, what do you want me to answer?" Perot asked, a little flustered.

"I wondered if you really are going to not give people [earning more than sixty thousand dollars a year] any Social Security benefits?"

Perot said he had never suggested such a thing, but that he would ask people like himself, "who just don't need" their Social Security benefits, to give them up "voluntarily." "I think there are many, many people who will say, 'If that will help, I'll give it up.'"

"Well, you can afford to give it up," Roberta said.

"That's the criteria, people who can afford to give it up."

"Who are those people, Mr. Perot?" Roberta asked.

"Let's go make the computer runs and define it," he said. "This is a rational analysis."[17]

As Perot found out, people can be tough interrogators when they feel their livelihoods are on the line. It has much more impact when a senior calls to ask about her benefits, or when an unemployed person asks what you're going to do to get him a job, than it does when Sam Donaldson or I ask about Social Security or unemployment. "Those of us who regard ourselves as hard news reporters do not have a copyright on asking good questions," Bernard Shaw says. "Some of the best questions in campaign '92 came from voters."[18]

Notes

1. *Congressional Quarterly Almanac, 102nd Session, 1992* (Washington, D.C.: Congressional Quarterly Inc., 1993), p. 6-A.

2. Times Mirror Center for the People & the Press, Washington, D.C.

3. Mario M. Cuomo, telephone interview with author, August 18, 1993.

4. Federal News Service transcript, March 18, 1992.

5. "Larry King Live," CNN, October 5, 1992.

6. James Carville, interview with author, May 25, 1993.

7. "Larry King Live," CNN, July 22, 1992.

8. Carville, interview.

9. Paul E. Tsongas, interview with author, May 14, 1993.

10. Mandy Grunwald, telephone interview with author, July 1, 1993.

11. Tim Russert, interview with author, August 3, 1993.

12. Gary Hart, telephone interview with author, May 12, 1993.

13. Ibid., May 17, 1993.

14. "Larry King Live," CNN, January 8, 1992.

15. John H. Sununu, interview with author, May 5, 1993.

16. Ross Perot, interview with author, May 17, 1992.

17. "Today," NBC, June 11, 1992.

18. Bernard Shaw, interview with author, May 25, 1993.

7

Politics Outweigh
the Media in Elections

Jeff Greenfield, interviewed by Liz Cunningham

Jeff Greenfield is a media critic and political analyst for the ABC News show Nightline. *Formerly a speechwriter, he is the author of several books, including* The Real Campaign. *Liz Cunningham is the author of* Talking Politics, *from which this viewpoint is taken.*

In 1992, the traditional media made a conscious decision to upgrade the quality of election and campaign coverage, and they were largely successful. However, neither the old media nor the new media were as important in determining the election results as were political and economic circumstances. For instance, Ross Perot's successfulness in the 1992 election was based more on his stance opposing "business-as-usual" politics than on the millions of dollars he spent on new media "infomercials." Elections always have been decided more on political ideology and economic matters than on use of the media.

In his book on the 1980 election, The Real Campaign, *Jeff Greenfield countered the widely held belief that Reagan's triumph was in large part due to the success of the Reagan campaign's image management tactics, arguing that Reagan was an ideological candidate, not an empty-headed actor.[1] Even Reagan's harshest critics now admit that Reagan's political clout primarily derived from an ideological mandate, not his skills as the Great Communicator.*

Twenty-five years of experience, as speechwriter and political consultant, media critic, and practitioner of journalism, have continually sharpened Greenfield's view of the influence of the press and political handlers. Covering the Clinton administration's travails during its first months in 1993 for Nightline, *Greenfield noted, with a taut reserve that belies his analytical zeal, "Odd as it may seem, political operatives and journalists, two professions usually thought of as hopelessly cynical, seem to be telling us the same thing: image and perception only go so far."[2]*

Cunningham: There was a lot of pressure to reform campaign coverage after 1988. What was done at ABC News in the way of reform?

Greenfield: What happened in 1988 was all the networks looked up and said, "We can't do this anymore." And I know that there was a very conscious decision here. We said, "We cannot cover campaigns the way we have been covering campaigns. We're prisoners of the campaign trail; we're prisoners of the thought of the day, of the canned comment—we've got to figure out a different way to cover campaigns." And all of the networks in 1992 did very different kinds of work, quite deliberately.

Paul Friedman, who is now executive vice president of ABC News, and [ABC News anchor] Peter Jennings, and [ABC News president] Roone Arledge, and [executive producer] Jeff Gralnick, planned a very deliberate way to go outside the mold—to assign beat reporters on things like health and the economy and housing and education, to look at the candidates' proposals and see whether or not they made sense. All the networks subjected the ads and debate claims and speech claims of the candidates to very rigorous—or attempted—very rigorous analysis to see how accurate or inaccurate they were.

Where campaigns are won or lost has a lot more to do with what's really out there in the world than how people campaign on the media.

What were the things you didn't like about the coverage before?

We'd been treating the campaign trail and the daily appearances of the candidates as the key news of the day and simply saying, "This is what candidate X said, and here's a sound bite," and "Here's what candidate Y said and here's a sound bite." Instead everybody decided to go outside of this mold, to go into communities where the candidates had been or were coming to, and talk to people about what they thought of the campaign relative to their own needs and worries and concerns. Try to take a step out of the campaign rhetoric and say, "What's the record of these candidates? What did Bill Clinton do in Arkansas? How did George Bush govern in four years?"

They would not let the candidates define and limit the parameters of what the coverage was. And if the candidates didn't want to talk about education, that didn't mean that a reporter couldn't go out and look at the record of the candidates and say something intelligent. When Ross Perot emerged, ABC did a one-hour special in which we took a look at different parts of Perot's career, his work at GM, his work on educational reform in Texas, a controversy about a particular development down in Dallas, and the POW issue. And then Perot came on after the local news and did a ninety-minute town meeting with Jennings and an audience.

Controversy over scandal coverage

Nightline *did a report on the media coverage of the Gennifer Flowers story in '92, just after the story broke [in January 1992]. The report was criticized as an example of the elite media picking up a sleazy story under the guise of "looking at the media coverage." What do you say to that criticism?*

That story is so widely misunderstood. We had endless debate that day as to whether to do that story, and we ultimately decided to do it because Bill Clinton and Hillary Clinton had tentatively agreed to come on *Nightline* that night and talk about it. That's why we did that story. Then they changed their mind at the last minute, either because of logistics or because they decided to do the *60 Minutes* interview.

We were left at nine o'clock at night with that story, whereupon Clinton's aide, Mandy Grunwald, being a very smart woman, beat the living daylights out of [*Nightline* anchor] Ted Koppel for doing the story. She basically excoriated us for "slipping into the gutter." But she made a quite powerful point that "why aren't we talking about health care, the economy, crime, foreign policy? Why are we wallowing in this?" And for one of the few times that I can ever remember, in the years I was on *Nightline*, Koppel was clearly on the defensive about this. . . . And that was, from a political point of view, very effective.

We had a story that we were going to do about the primary and the politics, and just very glancingly allude to Gennifer Flowers. Then we were told into the evening that Bill and Hillary wanted to come on and talk about this. So we geared up full speed to do that, and then they decided that they would rather do the *60 Minutes* interview, or maybe the weather was just too bad to get Clinton out or whatever . . . and there we were.

When you originally debated whether to devote the broadcast to the Flowers story, what were your major concerns?

The same concerns that Mandy Grunwald was raising. Is this what a mainstream journalistic organization should be doing at a critical point in a presidential campaign? Do we know whether Gennifer Flowers was telling the truth? Are we dragging this campaign into the gutter? All those were real concerns. But once the Clintons said, "Well, we'd like to come on and confront this," the issue's over. You don't debate that. You don't say to Bill and Hillary Clinton, "We really don't want you to come on *Nightline* and talk about this because it's unseemly." That's asking a little much of any newscast.

Excessive concern over talk shows

What do you think of the view that talk shows have a negative influence on campaigns, because they don't offer the scrutiny of candidates that traditional journalism does?

I think this is an excessive concern. My feeling is that as long as the old-fashioned journalists are free to cover candidates, to point out their weaknesses, to expose their deceits, we're OK. Sure, if you buy an ad or make a speech or go on a talk show where the host is less inquisitive, that's one way to get your message across, but nothing stops reporters, columnists, analysts from going on very well watched programs and saying, "Here's how this guy's lying" or "Here's how this guy's distorting the truth."

People do look at Perot's success in 1992 and think, "How could someone like Perot succeed without talk shows?"

I think Perot's success in 1992 was a measure of the really profound dissatisfaction with the political system. Now look, forget talk shows, the guy spent sixty million bucks on paid media mostly. I mean, that obviously had something to do with it. But somebody else could spend sixty million bucks and flop.

It wasn't just that Perot had money, although that was very important. It was that he seemed to be the exact response to the kind of politics people are fed up by—the evasive language, the compromises, the "business as usual." The reason why I think he did as well as he did was people just felt that in some sense some "radical bit of surgery was needed." It's not just that you have access to the public; it's what you are saying, and how does that fit the public sense of what's going on.

The limited influence of the media

How important do you think media relations are to a candidate's success?

I think the whole notion that what happens in the media is determinative of what happens in campaigns is to me a very suspect notion. I mean, you give George Bush an [economic] growth rate in 1992 of 3½ percent and you know, MTV and Larry King may matter a lot less. All of the stuff is important on the margins—it's not who wins and who loses. To me where campaigns are won or lost has a lot more to do with what's really out there in the world than how people campaign on the media.

In the book that I did on the 1980 campaign, *The Real Campaign*, what I had to say about that campaign has become conventional wisdom: that what Reagan had is what few presidents or American politicians have, a relatively coherent ideology. He ran on it and he'd spoken for it for twenty years before he got elected president. There's no clearer case of a guy who got elected with an ideological mandate in our recent history than Reagan.

The big shock in Washington was when Reagan got elected he proceeded to do precisely what he said he was going to do—huge defense buildup, big tax cut, try to get regulators off business's back. And whether that was the right or wrong policy, Reagan did what he said he was going to do. The argument of my book was that the press in covering all this stuff, in looking at the media, missed the fact that this was a very significant political decision by the country to change course dramatically. And the person who they were following was a guy who was one of the most clear-cut ideological candidates we have ever produced.

Now it was also true that he was weak on a lot of facts, that he was careless about what was real and what was fantasy. But this was an amazing campaign, very unusual for American politics, where a very clearly defined ideological candidate with a very clear set of policies was what people were responding to. They had made a political judgment that not only the incumbent administration but the whole direction of the country was politically wrong. And they wanted it to change dramatically and Reagan offered them that. That to me was what 1980 was about. Not whether or not Reagan looked good on television.

So you don't believe that Reagan's style of media management played a major role in his success?

I recounted all kinds of terrible Reagan mistakes on the air. They were reported, they were laughed at, they were featured in network newscasts. All kinds of media gaffes that we would consider devastating. And the reason why it didn't hurt Reagan was because people felt they knew who this guy was in a political sense. I think what they got, which I would regard as fundamentally accurate, was that this guy had a very firm—or if you didn't like him "rigid"—set of beliefs.

I think we've grown up in a time when both the press and the politicians believe that the media are the determinative factor. And my argument has always been that, well, it counts; you've got to pay attention to it, but it counts on the margins. It can do some things. It can get you well known; it'll help if you know how to use the media to convey a certain image, like Clinton's bus tour in the 1992 campaign.

But we're overrating it in terms of the campaign as well as in terms of governing. By and large, George Bush lost in 1992 because the economy was in really bad shape, because the Republicans lost three of the most important arguments they had been making to the voters in the last dozen or more years. They lost "foreign affairs strength," because things went too well and nobody cared. They lost "economic growth," not because of the media, but because the growth stopped. And they lost "taxes," because Bush felt he had to go back on that 1988 promise. Those factors are so much more important than how a candidate does or doesn't do on television that I think it's silly to talk about this as though media performance is the key to whether you win or lose.

When Bush ran against Dukakis, the Communist threat was still very real; the Reagan record on foreign affairs was pretty damn good overall. Bush had much more experience than Dukakis, an appeal that still mattered to people, and economic growth was chugging along. The fact that Dukakis rode in a tank didn't help him obviously. But look at where the country thought it was in 1988. By and large Reagan had done an effective job. Bush ran as Reagan's heir and Dukakis was seen as this guy that didn't really have a grip on the importance of foreign affairs and was out of touch with the values of a lot of Americans .

One of the things that Clinton did in 1992, and this isn't a media strategy nearly as much as it is a political strategy in the broader sense, is Clinton ran as a "pro–death penalty, tough on crime, end welfare as we know it, jobs and growth Democrat." Which hadn't been done for a while. But those are not media matters; those ought to be thought of, in my view, as political matters.

Media influence in past elections

Has there been in your mind a close presidential election in the last thirty years where media relations played an important role?

I think if you look at the 1976 Jimmy Carter–Gerald Ford race, even though neither of them were what you'd call "media stars," it made more of a difference there, because the issues were less dramatic. I think the fact that Carter was positioned as a kind of fairy tale, "man of the people, carries his own garment bag" man made a difference. But again, remember the overhang of 1976, coming out of Watergate. That was a very unusual political climate.

The other argument is that Ford closed as well as he did because his media campaign was very effective. He came from thirty points down and lost by about two. He had very effective advertising. His media campaign raised very effectively some doubts about Carter, that Carter was not a person of principle, that he did not have the breadth of experience necessary to run the country. And they communicated that message well, but it was in a context where there weren't great issues on the table.

When Carter tried to do that to Reagan—Carter ran the same kind of ads that Ford had run against him, describing Reagan as a "simplistic, trigger-happy, dangerous" kind of guy—it didn't work, because people really were sufficiently fed up with Carter to say, "We've got to get somebody else in here." And the Bush campaign tried much the same tactic against Clinton, but the political terrain was different and it didn't stick.

How a president or a candidate communicates and how they look on television matters, but it matters in context.

What about the accusation that Carter was really chewed up by the news media and that's one of the main reasons he lost in 1980?

I think that when you have a massive recession that cripples the industrial heartland of America, when you have inflation running at an annualized rate of as much as 20 percent in the spring of 1980, when your foes in the world appear to have taken the offensive, and when half of your own party is trying to dump you in favor of a challenger—I regard those as political rather than media problems, by and large.

The hostage thing is trickier. I would argue media made a difference in the Iranian Hostage Crisis. [In November 1979, Iranian militants seized the U.S. embassy in Tehran and held 51 people hostage for 444 days.] I think the fact that Walter Cronkite signed off every night by counting down the number of days that the hostages were in captivity, that the precursor to *Nightline*, called *America Held Hostage*, certainly elevated the Hostage Crisis to a level that in strict geopolitical terms it probably didn't deserve. But I would also argue that you had the complicity of the Carter administration. For its own political reasons it made the Hostage Crisis front and center. Carter refused to leave the White House, wouldn't light the Christmas tree star until the hostages were released. It was a joint effort to exaggerate the importance of the Hostage Crisis.

I get exasperated by this argument because it tends to put the stage above the play. And I think that's wrong. I heard once one person describe years ago the visit of John Paul II to Poland as a "media event." As though the return of the first Polish-born pope to his homeland would have been a nonevent if television hadn't been there! It's just not, in my view, what's at stake. Richard Nixon, who was one of the least "mediagenic" figures in American history, managed to spend four years in office and get reelected in what I believe was the single biggest margin of victory in American political history. What does that tell you?

My argument is not an absolutist argument. For instance, the televised debates in 1960 made a difference. Remember, when you have an election decided by one-tenth of 1 percent of the vote you can pretty well argue that anything hit the balance. Maybe it was Robert Kennedy's phone call to the jail where Martin Luther King, Jr., was. But I don't argue that the first time we had television debates in history and that seventy million people are watching and Nixon looks like he's about to die, that it doesn't have an impact. But you also need to remember that in 1968 Richard Nixon went into the general election leading Hubert Humphrey by fifteen points, outspent him two to one, and beat him by one point. Now how successful was that?

I mean, how important is the media compared to the fact that the Democratic party had been ripped to shreds by the argument over Vietnam in 1968 and the perception of a lot of the country was that, between Vietnam and domestic riots, the incumbent president had literally lost control of things? And how important was it that in a lot of key states George Wallace siphoned off millions of traditional Democratic votes? Where do you lay that stuff up, compared to whether or not Nixon had a better message in '68 than '60?

My argument is not that television doesn't matter. I would not advise, if I were still advising politicians, any politician running for president to forget the media. I would only say that the role it plays in elections needs to be put in its proper place. I think what goes into advertising and how a president or a candidate communicates and how they look on television matters, but it matters in context. It's not the be-all and end-all of campaigns. If you had given George Bush 4½ percent growth from January to November of 1992, he would have been almost certainly reelected and all the bus tours and all the "Arsenios" and all the "Larry Kings" and "MTVs" wouldn't have changed that.

Notes

1. Greenfield, Jeff, *The Real Campaign: How the Media Missed the Story of the 1980 Campaign* (New York: Summit Books, 1982), p. 23.

2. ABC News, *Nightline*, June 29, 1993.

8

The New Media Pose Hidden Dangers

Michael Schudson

Michael Schudson is a professor of communication and sociology at the University of California, San Diego, and a fellow at the Center for Advanced Study in the Behavioral Sciences. He is the author of several books on the news, popular culture, and politics, including The Power of News.

New media forms such as talk shows and electronic town meetings have the potential for improving political communication and democratizing presidential campaigns, but they could also prove dangerous. One danger is that people will use airing of their opinions on talk shows as a substitute for real action on the issues that concern them. Another danger is that politicians will use these electronic town meetings to manipulate public decisions while bypassing deliberative decision-making bodies, including Congress. Though many credit the new media with increasing voter participation in the 1992 election, participation will likely return to historically low levels.

Criticism of television's impact on democratic debate has given rise to a growing list of remedies: longer sound bites on the evening news, new procedures for making presidential debates more illuminating, more diverse broadcast formats for questioning candidates, even nationwide electronic town meetings. Refurbishing public discourse is a worthy cause, but will it cure the massive ills of modern democracy? Is the problem with our politics, at its root, a failure to communicate?

If these proposals were enacted and succeeded in expanding citizen participation in elections, they would be laudable. Still, they would do nothing to ensure that government is more responsible, responsive, and effective so that people would feel continuing reason to participate.

Historically low public participation

But, worse, carrying out these proposals would do little to increase citizen involvement. Even the most radical reform, the electronic town meeting,

Michael Schudson, "The Limits of Teledemocracy." Reprinted with permission from *The American Prospect*, Fall 1992; © New Prospect, Inc.

is unlikely to increase public participation in government. After the novelty wore off, such meetings probably would not attract a much larger audience than face-to-face town meetings, and the record of those is not encouraging.

In seventeenth-century Dedham, Massachusetts, town meeting attendance typically exceeded 70 percent, according to Jane Mansbridge's 1980 study, *Beyond Adversary Democracy*. But this impressive figure was attained only where every inhabitant lived within a mile of the meeting place, a town crier visited the house of each absentee half an hour into the meeting, fines were levied for absence or tardiness, and only some sixty men were eligible in the first place. In Sudbury, a town that imposed no fines, attendance averaged 46 percent during the 1650s. Overall, Mansbridge estimates that 20 to 60 percent of potential voters attended meetings in eighteenth-century Massachusetts.

As a substitute for politics, the new forms of direct teledemocracy could become quite dangerous.

Results from experiments in electronically mediated democratic forms are no more encouraging. F. Christopher Arterton, whose 1987 book *Teledemocracy: Can Technology Protect Democracy?* is the most comprehensive review of these experiments, finds "little support for the notion that citizens have the interest necessary to sustain near universal participation." Arterton concludes, "Most citizens, probably around two-thirds, will not participate."

These unsentimental assessments—something of a cold shower for teledemocracy—should not keep us from taking seriously ideas for improving the format and technology of democratic discourse. The proposed reforms of electioneering are based on the correct premise that different media and communicative settings affect the messages that get through. A kind of soft McLuhanism—not that the medium is the message, but that the medium shapes and constrains the message—is as sensible as [Marshall] McLuhan's determinism was absurd. Some grievances, some questions, some original solutions or proposals are more likely to emerge in particular media systems than in others.

The potential impact of media forms suggests a need for pluralism. What might we learn about our candidates, and about ourselves, through different media and varied formats? We don't know until we try.

New media, new publics

New forms of communication create different kinds of public discussion, and even different publics. Talk radio, for example, offers a striking contrast with traditional settings for public debate. The anonymity of the radio talk show format provides an occasion for many who might not feel comfortable speaking up at a PTA meeting. And the pressure on callers as well as host to be clever, knowing, and perhaps cynical often draws out a kind of exchange unheard at the PTA. It would be horrifying if this were the only model or dominant model of political discourse, but it is fine, perhaps bracing, that it is one among many forms of political talk available.

Some critics believe that no good can come of talk radio or an electronic meeting because they are not Greek agora or face-to-face town meetings in classic New England style. But face-to-face communication does not guarantee authenticity, nor do the electronic media preclude it. Sometimes, in fact, impersonal media improve communication. Many people have the experience of expressing something in a letter that they were unable to say face-to-face. One study some years ago found that middle-class people learned most about their children's school from face-to-face conversations with teachers, but working-class people typically learned more about the school from print and broadcast media. In teaching a lecture class of 400 students, I have found that when students could ask questions or engage in conversation with me by E-mail, I got much more comment (and, interestingly, on a first name basis!) than I ever had in face-to-face office hours.

So there are no grounds for automatic distrust of the newer and more mediated forms of communication. They open up new possibilities. As these examples suggest, they have a democratic effect, lowering the barriers that class and status set in the way of open communication.

I do not worry, as some have, that with Jerry Brown's 800 number, Ross Perot on Larry King, and Bill Clinton on Arsenio Hall and MTV, our presidential candidates have been reduced to mere entertainers. From the 1790s on, similar fears have animated American conservatives each time a party or candidate found a new way to address the people, especially the less politically active, more effectively than before. The most recent attempts to reach out to the disaffected and break through the conventional forms have improved political communication and helped democratize the practice of presidential campaigning.

Democratic delusions

As additions to the repertoire of political talk, the new media forms should be welcomed. But as a substitute for politics, the new forms of direct teledemocracy could become quite dangerous.

The dangers are of two kinds—the substitution of ritual for genuine politics and the creation of a form of direct democracy that short-circuits representative government. On the one side, there is the possibility that new forms of political communication will become a mere palliative, if there is no real chance government will act to remedy the problems the talk is about. On the other is the potential for manipulated public decision.

Ross Perot's proposal for nationwide electronic town meetings raises this second problem. Unlike other suggested reforms, Perot's aims not to enhance voting decisions or citizen communication with representatives but to replace the Congress with the direct plebiscitary decision making.

This takes up an old dream, or nightmare, of what democracy might be if we only had the technical capacity to register popular moods, morals, or preferences instantaneously. A century ago, [James] Lord Bryce envisioned a stage of history when the will of the majority might "become ascertainable at all times, and without the need of its passing through a body of representatives, possibly even without the need of voting machinery at all." Should this come to pass, then "public opinion would not only reign but govern." Today, with interactive cable systems and 800 numbers, the Brycean dream could become a reality. But is it a dream worth pursuing?

No, and certainly not in the vague form in which Ross Perot presented it. His vision seems to be Bonapartist—one leader, one people. "We go to the American people on television, explain it in great detail, and say, 'Here are the alternatives that we face. Which of these alternatives, as owners of the country, do you feel is best for the country?' The American people react, by congressional district, and we know what the people want."

The new formats supplement and enliven standard news practices. They do not replace them.

Who is the "we" in front of the public? It seems to be an imperial, or at least presidential, "we." Would different parties present different alternatives? Apparently not, not in the view of a man who scoffs at parties and thinks governing is just a matter of getting down to business.

Polling, whatever its many defects, has taught one clear lesson: the answer depends on the question. Even subtle differences in question-wording can have profound consequences for the answers people give. In short, those who determine the agenda set up the outcome. Electronic town meetings would not "tell us what the people want." They would tell us how a minority, the attentive public, answers questions framed by a president who, in Perot's system, would be a frighteningly strong leader. This is tell-a-democracy, or perhaps sell-a-democracy, not teledemocracy.

For Perot, as for too many others, public opinion consists of individual preferences and values; the task is simply to find a technique good enough to ascertain them. For most democratic theorists, on the other hand, public opinion consists of opinions formed in public, as people collectively face public issues; it is not a set of inclinations, grunts, and nods of approval and disapproval privately evolved and privately expressed to a pollster or voting machine. Democratic theory typically (and rightly) envisions a system of government organized as much to foster deliberation as to guarantee participation.

Perot's proposal for instantaneous mass decision making actually seems to have fewer safeguards than are available for important consumer decisions. People may have waiting periods (to buy a gun or to get a marriage license) or have to sign contracts in the presence of witnesses or may even have three days after pledging their fortunes to a door-to-door salesman to change their minds. All this helps ensure a level of serious consideration in private transactions. It would seem strange indeed to call for less rigorous protection for public deliberation.

No bypass

There is a delusion that sometimes accompanies talk of electronic democracy—that somehow citizens' direct communications with candidates will bypass the professional and obstructive news media. But even the best proposals, like James S. Fishkin's deliberative poll [a proposal sponsored by PBS and ten presidential libraries to televise the questioning of presidential candidates prior to the primary elections by a randomly selected nationwide group of people], depend mightily on the effective functioning of the professional news media. What Fishkin's deliberative opinion poll and Perot's electronic town meeting and talk radio and other proposals all lack is follow-up. When the town meeting is over, the stage returns to the candidates trailed by the press plane or press bus.

Recall Gerald Ford's 1976 presidential debate with Jimmy Carter and Ford's gaffe about the Soviet Union not dominating Poland (he was more right than he knew!). This remark was almost completely ignored by the general viewing audience. Two hours after the debate, viewers gave Ford a victory by 44 to 35 percent; but by noon the next day Carter was the winner 44 to 31, and by that evening Carter was judged the winner 61 to 19. What happened in the interim? The news professionals got into the act.

Now, perhaps the news media blew Ford's remark out of proportion. I am not arguing that what professional journalists provide is the best approximation to the truth. But they do offer constant scrutiny in a presidential campaign (this is much less true, regrettably, in state and local elections). With daily publication, they have the opportunity to monitor candidates over the long haul (and to monitor officials in office). Only a small percentage of the electorate actually saw Ross Perot on Larry King, or Bush or Clinton on the morning news shows. Most of us know about them thanks to the mainstream news media.

Regularly interacting with colleagues and politicians, the political reporters educate one another about politics in a way that sharpens their focus. This is not to say there are no dangers of media feeding frenzies and parochialism—those dangers are serious. It is not to say that news professionals do not have their own biases—they do. It is to claim that they represent a vital community of discourse—the best we have.

Proposals for more debates or better debate formats or "nine Sundays" of extended programs on presidential issues or longer sound bites on the evening news or wider use of talk radio and talk television or experiments with new formats and forums for presidential campaigning all stand some chance of keeping the news professionals more honest, forcing them to listen to voices and styles of discourse they do not control. The new formats supplement and enliven standard news practices. They do not replace them. They can contribute in modest ways to the quality of public discussion in presidential campaigns. But that discussion still comes most fully into focus in the mainstream press.

And that discussion still fundamentally depends on the two leading political parties and their candidates. The excitement of the 1992 campaign has much less to do with the communication experiments than with the unlikely prospect of a unified Democratic Party at a moment of Republican vulnerability. The possibility of a Democratic presidential victory for the first time in sixteen years, coupled with the substantive differences between the parties—on health care, education, industrial policy, and abortion and other social issues—generates the excitement. As always, it is the substance of politics that makes reforms in the framework of public debate worth thinking about.

Organizations to Contact

The editors have compiled the following list of organizations concerned with the issues debated in this book. The descriptions are derived from materials provided by the organizations. All have publications or information available for interested readers. The list was compiled on the date of publication of the present volume; names, addresses, and phone numbers may change. Be aware that many organizations take several weeks or longer to respond to inquiries, so allow as much time as possible.

Accuracy in Media (AIM)
4455 Connecticut Ave. NW, Suite 330
Washington, DC 20008
(202) 371-6710
fax: (202) 371-9054

AIM is a conservative media watchdog organization. It researches public complaints on errors of fact made by the news media and requests that such errors be corrected publicly. It publishes the semimonthly *AIM Report* and a weekly syndicated newspaper column.

American Society of Newspaper Editors (ASNE)
PO Box 4090
Reston, VA 22090-1700
(703) 648-1144
fax: (703) 620-4557

The society consists of editors in charge of major policy decisions at American daily newspapers. It publishes the *American Society of Newspaper Editors— Bulletin* nine times a year and various research reports, manuals, handbooks, and brochures.

Center for Investigative Reporting (CIR)
568 Howard St., 5th Floor
San Francisco, CA 94105-3008
(415) 543-1200
fax: (415) 543-8311

The center is a small nonprofit journalism organization dedicated to in-depth investigative reporting. It produces investigative reports, offers consulting services to news and special-interest organizations, and conducts workshops and seminars for investigative journalists. It publishes the quarterly *Muckraker: Journal of the Center for Investigative Reporting.*

Center for Media and Public Affairs (CMPA)
2101 L St. NW, Suite 300
Washington, DC 20037
(202) 223-2942
fax: (202) 872-4014

CMPA is a research organization that studies the media's treatment of social and political affairs and uses surveys to measure the media's influence on public opinion. It publishes the monthly *Media Monitor* and *Political Newswatch* newsletters and numerous books, including *Good Intentions Make Bad News: Why Americans Hate Campaign Journalism.*

Center for Media Literacy
1962 S. Shenandoah St.
Los Angeles, CA 90034
(310) 559-2944
fax: (310) 559-9396

The center is a media education organization that seeks to give the public power over the media by fostering media literacy. It produces media literacy workshop kits that include educational videos and booklets and publishes the quarterly *Connect.*

Fairness and Accuracy in Reporting (FAIR)
130 W. 25th St.
New York, NY 10001
(212) 633-6700
fax: (212) 727-7668

FAIR is a liberal media watchdog organization that seeks to expose conservative bias in the media. It publishes the bimonthly *EXTRA!* magazine and *Extra! Update* newsletter in alternate months and produces the nationally syndicated weekly radio program *CounterSpin.*

Freedom Forum Media Studies Center
Columbia University
2950 Broadway
New York, NY 10027-7004
(212) 280-8392

The center is a research institute for the advanced study of mass communication and technological change. It sponsors workshops, seminars, and research on the effects of the media on society. The center publishes the quarterly *Media Studies Journal* as well as numerous conference reports and papers, including *The Media and Campaign '92: A Series of Special Election Reports.*

Kettering Foundation
200 Commons Rd.
Dayton, OH 45459-2799
(513) 434-7300
fax: (513) 439-9804

The foundation is a nonprofit research institution that studies problems of community, governing, politics, and education, with a particular focus on deliberative democracy. It publishes the quarterlies the *Kettering Review* and *Connections* newsletter as well as the National Issues Forum book series.

MediaWatch
517 Wellington St. W., Suite 204
Toronto, ON M5V 1G1
CANADA
(416) 408-2065
fax: (416) 408-2069

MediaWatch is a feminist organization that monitors media bias toward women in politics. It produces research papers on the representation of women in advertising and the media.

Media Watch
PO Box 618
Santa Cruz, CA 95061-0618
(408) 423-6355

This feminist organization monitors and organizes campaigns against bias and violence toward women that appear in the media. It publishes the quarterly newsletter *Action Agenda* and produces educational videos on media bias.

Times Mirror Center for the People and the Press
1875 I St. NW, Suite 1110
Washington, DC 20006
(202) 293-3126

The center conducts opinion surveys and studies on the attitudes of the public, the media, and politicians toward political and media issues. It publishes numerous research reports, including *The People, the Press, and Their Leaders*.

Twentieth Century Fund
41 E. 70th St.
New York, NY 10021
(212) 535-4441

This research foundation sponsors analysis of economic policy, foreign affairs, and domestic political issues. It publishes numerous books and the report *1-800-PRESIDENT: The Report of the Twentieth Century Fund Task Force on Television and the Campaign of 1992*.

Bibliography

Books

Stephen Ansolabehere, Roy Behr, and Shanto Iyengar	*The Media Game: American Politics in the Television Age.* New York: Macmillan, 1993.
David Croteau	*By Invitation Only: How the Media Limit Political Debate.* Monroe, ME: Common Courage Press, 1994.
Richard Davis	*Politics and the Media.* Englewood Cliffs, NJ: Prentice Hall, 1994.
Suzanne Garment	*Scandal: The Crisis of Mistrust in American Politics.* New York: Times Books, 1991.
Jack W. Germond and Jules Witcover	*Mad as Hell: Revolt at the Ballot Box, 1992.* New York: Warner Books, 1993.
Doris A. Graber, ed.	*Media Power in Politics.* 3rd ed. Washington, DC: CQ Press, 1994.
Kathleen Hall Jamieson	*Packaging the Presidency: A History and Criticism of Presidential Campaign Advertising.* New York: Oxford University Press, 1992.
Douglas Kellner	*Media Culture: Cultural Studies, Identity, and Politics Between the Modern and the Postmodern.* New York: Routledge, 1995.
Matthew Robert Kerbel	*Edited for Television: CNN, ABC, and the 1992 Presidential Campaign.* Boulder, CO: Westview Press, 1994.
Matthew Robert Kerbel	*Remote and Controlled: Media Politics in a Cynical Age.* Boulder, CO: Westview Press, 1995.
S. Robert Lichter, Linda S. Lichter, and Stanley Rothman	*Prime Time: How TV Portrays American Culture.* Washington, DC: Regnery, 1994.
Thomas E. Mann and Garry R. Orren	*Media Polls in American Politics.* Washington, DC: Brookings Institution, 1992.
Thomas E. Mann and Norman J. Ornstein, eds.	*Congress, the Press, and the Public.* Washington, DC: American Enterprise Institute/Brookings Institution, 1994.
Michael Parenti	*Inventing Reality: The Politics of News Media.* New York: St. Martin's Press, 1993.
Jay Rosen and Paul Taylor	*The New News v. the Old News: The Press and Politics in the 1990s.* New York: Twentieth Century Fund Press, 1992.

Tom Rosenstiel	*Strange Bedfellows: How Television and the Presidential Candidates Changed American Politics, 1992*. New York: Hyperion, 1993.
Larry J. Sabato	*Feeding Frenzy: How Attack Journalism Has Transformed American Politics*. New York: Free Press, 1991.
Twentieth Century Fund Task Force on Television and the Campaign of 1992	*1-800-PRESIDENT: The Report of the Twentieth Century Fund Task Force on Television and the Campaign of 1992*. New York: Twentieth Century Fund Press, 1993.
Paul H. Weaver	*News and the Culture of Lying*. New York: Free Press, 1994.

Periodicals

Peter Andrews	"The Press," *American Heritage*, October 1994.
Ken Auletta	"On the Presidency and the Press," *Columbia Journalism Review*, November/December 1994.
Carl Bernstein	"Talk Show Nation," *New Perspectives Quarterly*, Summer 1994.
Gloria Borger	"Cynicism and Tankophobia," *U.S. News & World Report*, June 5, 1995.
Edwin Diamond, Martha McKay, and Robert Silverman	"Pop Goes Politics: New Media, Interactive Formats, and the 1992 Presidential Campaign," *American Behavioral Scientist*, November 1993. Available from Sage Publications, 2455 Teller Rd., Thousand Oaks, CA 91320.
James Fallows	"The Media's Rush to Judgment," *Washington Monthly*, January/February 1994.
James S. Fishkin	"Talk of the Tube: How to Get Teledemocracy Right," *American Prospect*, Fall 1992. Available from PO Box 383080, Cambridge, MA 02238.
Adam Gopnik	"Read All About It," *New Yorker*, December 12, 1994.
Janine Jackson	"Sex, Polls, and Campaign Strategy: How the Press Misses the Issues of the '92 Election," *Extra!* June 1992.
Kenneth Jost	"Political Scandals," *CQ Researcher*, May 27, 1994. Available from 1414 22nd St. NW, Washington, DC 20037.
Kenneth Jost	"Talk Show Democracy," *CQ Researcher*, April 29, 1994.
Morton Mintz	"Stories the Media Miss," *Washington Monthly*, March 1995.
Jim Naureckas	"We Want the Airwaves," *In These Times*, April 17, 1995.
Michael Nelson	"The Press and the President: How the Press Views the President," *Current*, October 1994.
Jay Rosen	"Journalism and the Production of the Present," *Tikkun*, September 1994.
George Stephanopoulos	"Is There a Liberal Bias in the Media?" *New Perspectives Quarterly*, Spring 1995.

Index